Dreams Beyond Dreaming

Dreams Beyond Dreaming

jean campbell

A UNILAW LIBRARY BOOK
The Donning Company/Publishers
Virginia Beach/Norfolk

Library of Congress Cataloging in Publication Data:

Campbell, Jean, 1943-
Dreams beyond dreaming.
1. Dreams.   I. Title.
BF1078.C28   154.6'3   79-26131
ISBN 0-89865-014-3
ISBN 0-89865-015-1 pbk.

Printed in the United States of America

To Leonard

Contents

Introduction

I guess I always believed that dreams and ESP were almost synonymous, for though my own childhood dreams have fled from memory, I grew up with the story of my mother's dream of Joe during World War II.

It was morning, she said, and she had drifted back to sleep when she saw in a dream her favorite younger brother, Joe, wounded in the leg by a sniper's bullet and then captured. He was in the infantry, fighting in Germany.

Two days later the telegram came. Joe had been wounded and captured.

To me this story, which in real life took place around my second birthday, was always as real as the stories my mother told of having been born with a caul, part of the placenta remaining attached to her forehead, and the old wives' tales of how that signified a child who was psychic.

It was not that my family put much stock in things psychic, nor was it a subject much discussed during my Catholic girlhood. Yet for me, there were other incidents which left me faintly curious, feeling that there was something left unexplained, which constant reading of myths and fairy tales did nothing to alleviate—like the time when around age four, and with a high fever connected with one of the childhood diseases, I was put down to sleep on my parents' big bed downstairs. Around the ceiling I noticed a swarm, if one could call it that, of darting, flying, tiny winged creatures like human beings with wings. They were products of my fever, I was told.

And again, about that same time, I awoke one morning to tell my mother that I had flown downstairs the night before. How vividly I remember the joy of swooping down the stairs, landing at the bottom, only to pick myself up and do it all over again. You were only dreaming, I was told, and everyone had a good laugh.

The "only dreaming" part, I'm sure, must have stuck, and I remembered very little else about my dreams until, shortly before my twenty-fourth birthday, I had two dreams which made the vividly insistent impression upon me that I should pay attention to them and to the rest of my dream life. It was not only the dreams themselves, but the feeling they evoked that something important was missing in my life. These are the dreams:

> #1: I was part of a tribal society, a young, teenage girl. I was chosen along with two others to be part of a rite which included the sacrificial murder of a fat and ugly old man. We went to the man's hut where he slept and, with a knife shaped like a scimitar, murdered him by plunging the blade into his belly. The rest of the tribe watched.
>
> Part of the ritual was that we three young girls were to be murdered in turn. I returned alone to my family's hut where my father sat outside the door. I entered the room and on a counter there was a metal post about twelve inches high with four strings attached. The strings stretched out perpendicular to the post and the ends of three of the strings encircled eggs. The fourth string held an empty circle. My mother entered the hut and I began to cry that I didn't want to die in the lye bath.
>
> #2: I was speaking with my mother at the kitchen table. Outside a uniformed maid washed the windows and in the basement my husband, the professor, hammered out a silver shield on which was engraved the mystic rose. While he hammered he invoked the name of Simon Transmagistrus.

With these two dreams I embarked on a voyage of discovery that was to take me into the as yet uncharted depths of the mystery of the human consciousness. When I began I had heard of Carl Jung only as someone who also knew Sigmund Freud and Wilhelm Reich. My knowledge of psychology existed only in the rudimentary form dispensed to college education majors and what flights of fancy my inquisitive post-college reading had taken me upon; and my exploration of dream literature leading to the world of metaphysics had not yet begun. Where else could I start but by looking at my own dreams?

I read and read in an attempt to interpret them, but I found then, as I believe now, that books written on the subject of dreams barely scratch the surface of a subject which I now know, after years of listening to dreams, discussing dreams, interpreting dreams, covers an area as broad as any of us can imagine—and as meaningful.

Chapter One

What To Do With A Dream

My own knowledge of what to do with a dream came slowly, albeit painlessly; and, as there are literally hundreds of books which deal with the subject of how to find a dream and keep it, let me dispense as quickly as possible with some of the basic techniques and get on to the material which I consider for one thing more fun, but for another potentially more practical.

The first and most important thing in recalling dreams is the wish to recall them. For myself, I gave the impetus of the two dreams recorded in the introduction to this book. For some, it's a belief that dreams can be useful—as a psychological tool in self-understanding, as a stimulus to creativity, as a way to deal with fears or solve problems. For others it's a belief that dreams can be fun or enjoyable. But that's the beginning, for dreams seldom come unbidden whether or not the waking self knows they are called for; and they seldom stay away, whether or not the waking self thinks it is wishing for a dream with all its heart.

If the desire to dream is there, then the waking self will encourage the dream self like a toddler being taught how to walk, for in fact in most cases that is exactly what the dream self is—in Western society a neglected stepchild, treated at best as if it were unimportant and at worst as thoroughly negligible. Oh, it was only a dream, or it must have been something you ate.

There are many ways to encourage the neglected dream child:

1. Get a notebook for recording dreams or, as a friend of mine likes to say, get the finest, most expensive

notebook you can find. Make a cover for it. Make it
beautiful and uniquely your own.

2. Keep the dream book with a pen or pencil at your
bedside. If you sleep with someone who wakes easily,
keep a penlight or a pen with a built-in light.

3. Keep a glass of water by the bed so that you can
sip it when awakening to keep from going back to sleep
before the dream is recorded. One of my friends, a psychic, prays that this glass of pure water he puts by his
bed each night will be filled with blessings of love and
light and illuminating dreams; and if the water is not
drunk by morning, he finishes it then.

4. Program the remembrance of dreams by repeating to yourself during the day or just before going to
sleep, I will remember my dreams clearly and completely until they are written down.

5. If you have the heart to try it, set the clock at
two-or three-hour intervals during the night to catch
the elusive dream periods that scientists call REM or
rapid eye movement periods when they believe dreams
to be closest to the surface.

6. Begin writing when you awaken. Don't wait
until you've had your morning coffee or a conversation
with someone else in the house.

7. Write down whatever comes into your head. You
might start with a feeling or a color or a single word.
Dreams can be elusive and some people remember only
feelings at first, but follow the feeling or the single
image and you may be surprised at what you come up
with.

Personally I never had any trouble once the first dreams im-
pinged on my waking consciousness. It was as if the floodgate had
burst and my problem was not recalling too few dreams, but *too
many*, and what to do with the wild assortment of scenes and
images that floated through my memory the moment I awakened,
sometimes four, five, and six dreams a night where people I then
knew and people I'd known before and sometimes people I'd never
seen, met in scenes that came from no waking memory. I knew, or
thought I knew, they must all have something to do with me; but
what? And how to determine what and what to do with it?

I began to read and to question other people about their
dreams. I soon learned that dreams contained symbols. In other
words, the messages were not always clear-cut and they meant more
than seemed apparent on the surface.

I started with the professor in the basement hammering out
the silver shield. At a friend's suggestion I read Carl Jung's autobiographical work *Memories, Dreams and Reflections* and learned

that for Jung in a series of dreams he had, the house symbolized the soul or the whole person and various areas of the house implied various areas of the personality. My dream became clearer. The maid was washing windows. Obviously I was cleaning the view into myself where I, along with my mother talked in the kitchen, that part of the house which represents the essence of feminine creativity.

From Jung I also learned about the collective unconscious, that area in which he believed all consciousness to be united so that memories which were apparently inaccessible, such as racial memories or information of which we had no conscious knowledge, became accessible. I learned his terms *animus* and *anima* representing respectively the male component of any female and the female component of any male which appeared in dreams.

Thus I discovered that my *animus*, the professor, the male part of myself to whom I was married, was in the basement, the subterranean levels of my mind, cooking up a surprise. And what a collective unconscious surprise it was.

Until that dream I had never consciously encountered the mystic rose, let alone known what it represented, and only my ongoing interest in symbology and mythology kept me looking. At the time I simply drew the symbol, three ovals intersecting one another like the contemporary symbols for nuclear energy with half-circles connecting the tops of the three interpenetrated circles making a circle with twelve points. From later study of the tarot, and early Christian symbolism, I discovered this twelve-pointed figure to be a symbol of Christian love, and even earlier to be representational of the power of the number 12 signified by the signs of the Zodiac.

The professor invoked the name of Simon Transmagistrus, and until I read Jung I had never heard of the ancient alchemist Hermes Trismegestus, who seems to appear here along with, quite possibly, the Christian Simon/Peter who learned mastery (Transmagistrus) through the love of Jesus.

By the time I had finished reading Jung, not only his autobiography which I recommend, but many of his scholarly works, which I do not, I had not only had a clearer insight into the nature of my dreams, but had also discovered the secret that Jung seemed to keep so well hidden from himself throughout most of his life, that it is impossible to fit the types of psychic experiences that he continued to have such as encounters with ghosts and foreknowledge of events, into the framework of traditional science and that attempts to do so may lead to the uncomfortable type of near schizophrenic behavior in which he often seemed to find himself. This peaked my interest in what we call the psychic, but that must be left for a later chapter as this is one on what to do with a dream.

What not to do with a dream is to take out all the books in the library that discuss the meanings of dream symbols and begin to follow them to the letter.

From books such as these we find that a symbol such as a snake in a dream means sex and that, dependent on what the snake is doing, we will find out our attitudes toward sex; and that a horse in a dream is a beast of burden, or as Plato recounted the horse may signify the passions, and nothing else.

What such dream symbol dictionaries as these do is parenthesize, box-in, the wealth of layers of personal symbolism available in any dream, making it again *only* a dream; and though such dictionaries may be used as a starting point, the serious explorer, wanting to find out the nature and meaning of inner reality, will never stop there.

From the dream dictionary I learned about my first dream that the knife is a sexual symbol and from Freud I learned that I might be wanting to symbolically kill my repressive father, but it was not until much later when I learned through the books of an expert dream analyst, Ann Faraday, and her teacher, Fritz Perls, that through the technique of gestalting a dream I could let the characters in my dream of ritual execution speak for themselves and reveal my own inner symbolism of desire to be "out with the old and in with the new."

What is *gestalting* a dream? The word *gestalt* itself means a total environment or the environment which surrounds an event, and *gestalting* a dream is a technique for achieving a total picture of the dream's meaning.

Let me take for an example the symbols found in the first of the two dreams found in the introduction. Although the symbolism of the tribal rite of killing the old, fat man became fairly clear immediately upon studying traditional dream literature, two other symbols in the dream remained a mystery until I was introduced to the idea of *gestalting* in which one becomes the dream symbol instead of just observing it.

As soon as I became the metal post in the dream, I began to describe myself. "I am a sturdy metal structure to which strings are attached. Even though one would think the eggs would weigh my strings down, they don't because they are bouyant eggs, almost ready to hatch and fly away. There are four strings because four is a stable number. The fourth string is empty because I am incomplete. The fourth egg is there, but it is not yet visible."

At once, speaking as the metal post, I gained a new insight into myself. The second symbol which was at first unclear to me, the lye bath, became clear as I understood this to be a play on words with lye substituting for lie. A deeper meaning was uncovered however, when I *became* the lye bath and understood that to be the portion of myself which scours away lies, just as a bath in lye would melt skin away from bones. In a later dream I found myself dumping a large, heavy sack of garbage (my own, I assume) into a lye pit.

Dream symbols are personally yours. You would not have selected particular elements for appearance on the dream stage or remembered particular dream events if they did not in some way connect with you. That is not to say they cannot connect with someone or something else, but you are the dreamer and thus the particular individual making the selection. Certainly dream symbols can have an overall meaning, a collective meaning, but their meaning is also personal. There are several techniques available for gestalting dreams but here are a few most commonly in use, which should help you if you truly want to investigate your own personal messages to yourself:

1. Find a group of people who are interested in working with dreams. For the beginner in dream interpretation this can often be the most helpful and quickest path to understanding since, for one thing, it is much easier to understand that your own dreams are not "crazy" or "stupid" or "insignificant" in the light of what you will find other people's dreams to be.

There are few ground rules to assume if you enter one of these groups or even if, not finding an already established group, you decide to establish one of your own. Never assume that someone else knows more about your dreams than you do yourself. In every dream group there seems to be at least one person who has been at it longer, has read more, and tends to see him/herself as an authority not only on personal dreams, but is glad to give an interpretation of everyone else's dream. If you fall for this, though the interpretation may sound logical, intelligent, better than anything you could imagine, it is just that—someone else's interpretation of your dream.

Yet the dream group can be invaluable for the person who wants to understand dream analysis. Why? Because so often we are crafty and, left to our own devices, will gloss over or simply dismiss the most important point of a dream.

2. Within a dream group, one *gestalting* technique is to listen as a group to one individual's dream, and then as a group apply the questioning technique. The technique is that the dreamer can

become any character or object in the dream that he or the group chooses.

Once the dreamer enters into the character of the dream role, the group begins to ask questions which the dreamer must answer always using the first person singular "I" such as "describe yourself," "how old are you," "what color are you," etc.

3. One technique which is sometimes effective to use in *gestalting* within a group is to have the dreamer change chairs or positions in the room when becoming some aspect of the dream.

The purpose of this technique, as well as the questioning, is that the dreamer begins to see the dream event from the perspective of the person or object in the dream instead of the perspective generally called "I." If it is true that we pick and choose the elements of the dream world as personal symbols, then in some sense of the word, the elements of the dream world are all parts of ourself, though they are parts which we ordinarily do not call "I" or "me."

Witness the dream of a girl who attended one of my creative dreaming seminars. It was early in the seminar and I was asking about recurring dreams from childhood, dreams which for the adult dreamer once seemed to hold a great deal of power, but were no longer part of the dream vocabulary.

The girl told the following recurring dream: "I am pushing my doll buggy when suddenly I am pushed from behind and the doll buggy with my favorite doll in it goes rolling down the hill that leads to the street. I scream and wake up." When asked if she knew who pushed her or why, she said no, but that as a child she had repeatedly dreamed this dream.

The group asked her to assume the role of the doll carriage, first describing herself. She was, she said, a very beautiful doll buggy indeed, a Paris model bought for the child by her parents.

When we asked the doll carriage if it knew who had pushed the little girl, since the push had come from behind her, it readily answered, "Yes." The assailant was a little boy, somewhat older than the little girl, who had terrified and tormented all the children on the block.

Though the girl did not know what had happened to the doll carriage after it left her hands and began to roll toward the street, the doll carriage itself answered us that it had tipped over before it ever reached the street and that the doll inside was thrown out, but both were unharmed.

Further questioning of the various elements of the dream

revealed that this recurring nightmare had taken place during a particularly unsettling period of the girl's childhood and that, though the dreams eventually ceased, the little boy in the dream represented certain attitudes toward the male sex which the girl still held, whereas the doll carriage represented her own self.

The gestalting of the dream became quite an emotional event for the girl and the support of the workshop group, many of whom she knew well, was helpful to her in recognizing and dealing with the old fears she still held.

4. One rule of thumb to recall when helping another person to *gestalt* a dream is to be sensitive to the nuances of emotion. As most people, including experienced dream interpreters, tend to think of the elements of the dream as quite distinct from "self," the attitude with which the dreamer regards particular dream elements may be the clue to deciding which element of an elaborate dream should be allowed to speak first. For example, one female dreamer reported a dream of her husband bringing in fireplace logs and stacking them in a corner by the fireplace. This was one of these dreams which dreamers so often call "inconsequential," and which "makes no sense." However, there was a certain emotional tone in her voice when she told of her husband stacking the logs. She was asked to assume the role of one of the logs and randomly chose one near the bottom of the pile.

Asked to describe herself as the log, she talked about being a tree growing in the woods and her feelings of usefulness when cut down as firewood. Sadly, however, our dreamer, as a fireplace log said that she seemed to be very near the bottom of the pile and was never, never used.

When asked if this dream represented her feelings toward herself, the dreamer admitted that indeed it did though she had tried hard to hide these feelings from herself. With the help of the dream group she was able to explore the problem and even search for some alternative solutions including dreaming about it.

5. Once people in a group are familiar with the technique of *gestalting* a dream it is often easier and more convenient to break into pairs or small groups for dream work. Yet even without the help of a group the *gestalt* technique is valid and can be used by recording the imagined conversations between various dream elements along with the dream itself in your dream journal.

How do you know if you're reading the symbols correctly?

Since at one level dreams are messages from the interior of ourselves to the exterior of ourselves, it is almost impossible *not* to know if the symbols are being interpreted correctly. We begin to grow. We begin to know more about ourselves and our relationship to the world around us.

However, any growth can be frightening as well as exciting, so one way to know if you're understanding your dreams is if you stop remembering them. This is not at all an unusual occurrence.

Many people have reported to me that the minute they began to record their dreams or otherwise take them seriously, the dreams stopped. Patience and persistence are the only answers I know to this problem. As I said earlier, we tend to be quite crafty with ourselves and the question of how much we really want to know about what we are thinking and feeling can be a difficult one to answer. Chances are that you do want to know yourself much better than you now do, but fear of what will come up can throw up roadblocks at least momentarily.

Some people will dream vigorously for several weeks or months, recording and analyzing every dream when, just as it seems the solution to a particular problem or the answer to a question is near, once again the dreams stop coming.

Again, do not be too concerned about this. Even in waking life we take vacations, give ourselves an occasional rest, and give things time to settle into quiet routine again.

A man in one of my dream workshops dreamed repeatedly for over a year about battle scenes until finally he realized that he was at war with himself and that if he would explore and determine his true feelings he would not have to wage these nightly battles. Elated, he waited for another type of dream to appear—but for several weeks nothing, even though he had been recalling several vivid dreams each night. Worrried, he turned to the dream group. Had he been incorrect in his assessment of the meaning of his dreams?

Finally, another dream came. Once again he was on the battlefield, but this time he entered the camp's infirmary. He was writing a letter home. This dream, with the contents of his letter to himself brought new understanding, and a new place from which to grow.

Repeated dream symbols can often be the clue to understanding the deepest levels of ourselves, which is why keeping a dream record can be doubly important, even though it sometimes seems dull and a waste of time. After you have kept a dream diary for a few months, try going back through your dream record and underlining those symbols which appear repeatedly.

I discovered one of my own important symbols after a major crisis in my life during which I felt often depressed and almost suicidal. The dream was as follows:

> I found myself in a walled garden, a courtyard tiled with small mosaic tiles. On the floor of the courtyard was the symbol for nuclear power, circles intertwined. I heard a voice saying, "The yellow bird is not dead." Then I was on a Grecian couch, a young dark-haired girl, and there was a man, a professor, sitting beside me. I felt as if I were both people at once. A man came out of the door of the villa behind us and said something to the professor. The professor said, "She will get well."

When I looked at the dream diaries I had kept for the two years prior to this dream, I found many other dreams where birds appeared, where I was feeding the birds or talking to them, something I had never considered to be of much importance because in waking life I am also fond of birds and have often watched birds and kept bird feeders.

Yet when I examined the hopeful message in this dream, I discovered that not only did the bird signify my fondness for winged creatures, but that birds seemed to be my own private symbol for my creative, happy, inner self or soul.

Examined carefully this same dream has two other symbols which recur in my own dreams and which both appeared in the dream discussed in the introduction to this book—that of the three interlaced circles and the professor. The circles, or the mystic rose, which appear at infrequent but always important intervals in my dreams, seem to represent power. The professor, of course, fulfills a role in the dream world much as he does in waking reality. It was not unusual for me to dream of schools or professors since I am myself a teacher.

In fact I was amused to discover as I reread my dreams I quite frequently dreamed of myself as a student or inmate in a school for retarded children, a state I put down to the fact that I knew several people who taught special education classes and also knew their students. However, as time went on, I recalled, with some satisfaction, a dream of being told by a teacher that I was well enough to leave this special education situation; and thereafter, as I went through my dream books, I had successively dreamed of myself as a child in an ordinary school, then a university student, and finally as a teacher myself. Learning to recognize these dreams, I came to call them progress reports, or dreams in which I reported to myself my own progress in self-understanding.

Another friend of mine, who was somewhat timid, had a similar succession of dreams in which she dreamed first of arriving at the train station too late and missing the train, losing timetables, etc.; then of catching the train, but encountering unpleasant people and unpleasant situations; and finally, of catching the train with a pleasant aftermath.

She progressed through these dreams as she underwent psychological counseling which aided her in waking life to become less timid and more outgoing.

Dream symbols, as we have seen here, come in many layers and many forms from the very simple to the very complex. In fact, you may well find that your dream vocabulary seems to grow with you; and that, inventively, as you are introduced to new ways of interpreting dreams, so will your dreams use corresponding symbols. The dreamer unfamiliar with Carl Jung's concept of the collective unconscious may have never recalled a dream which used anything but familiar, everyday objects and people. Yet once introduced to Jung, unfamiliar symbols appear quite by magic. The individual unacquainted with say, the mysteries of the Kabalah, may never think to use numbers as symbols in dreams; yet once acquainted with numbers may find them cropping up everywhere. This is certainly one of the more enjoyable characteristics of dream study.

A final way in which our dreams give us clues is with words or plays on words. Richard, who says he likes to have his messages straight instead of difficult to interpret, is very fond of the well-known St. Francis of Assissi. Interestingly enough, he also grew up in the town of St. Francis, and when he dreams dreams of a spiritual nature or messages about his spiritual growth, they are invariably located in St. Francis.

There, in his dream town, he encounters various people of his past and present acquaintance who give him messages by nature of their names. For example, a man by the name of Hunt may indicate that the dreamer is hunting for something. A friend by the name of Moore may indicate that he needs more of something and indicate what by what is begin carried or given.

What is more, Richard led himself to this method of dream interpretation by way of conscious decision. He decided that he did not want to have to work through a trial and error method of deciding what a dream meant, and programmed himself while he was awake by telling himself that he would dream dreams which were easy to interpret accurately.

Which leads us directly to the question of how much control we have over our dreams.

Chapter Two

Lucid Dreaming

On October 8, 1973, after several months of trying, I recorded my first lucid dream:

> It was bright moonlight and I was looking directly at the wings of a blue jay silhouetted against the moon. Suddenly I realized, I am flying. I'm dreaming. I did it! I did it! I looked at my hands just like Don Juan said and then away and back at the bluejay.

Since that time I have spoken with several people who, when asked if they are aware they are dreaming when they're dreaming, reply, "Of course;" and give me a look that implies, "Doesn't everyone do that?"

But in fact, if you are one of those people, most people are apparently not aware of the fact that they're dreaming as the dream goes on and often proceed with all sorts of bizarre antics during their dreams, only to wake up and recall they were dreaming. This state of being aware of dreaming as the dream occurs has come to be called *lucid dreaming* in the dream literature and, up to now, has generally been sandwiched into the end of the book, if mentioned at all, along with other dream oddities such as the precognitive dream, much as courses in modern American history so often start with the Industrial Revolution only to reach the present during the last week of class. It is another corollary of the "you were only dreaming" theorem.

I first encountered the idea of lucid dreaming in Carlos Castaneda's magnificent description of a Yaqui Indian sorcerer, Don Juan, in *Tales of Power*. The first book in the series *The Teachings of Don Juan* and, to date, three succeeding books, have been described by some critics as a sham and the writing of Castaneda, an American anthropology professor, as contrived and designed only to make money. I do not attempt to judge who is right in this matter, only that if what Castaneda says Don Juan says is true, then it should work.

In *Tales of Power* Don Juan tells Carlos that there is dreaming and there is *dreaming*. You are only dreaming, he says, until you learn to control the dream reality and do with it what you will, such as travel to places you wish to go in a time frame that is recognizable as ordinary waking reality.

This is not easy, Don Juan tells Carlos, and you must practice, first by realizing that you are dreaming when you are dreaming, and then by learning how to stabilize the dream world.

Don Juan teaches Carlos the technique of first realizing that he is dreaming and then looking at his hands (or any other things you always carry with you, Don Juan says) and then away at some object in the dream, then back at his hands and so on, ever increasing the scope of vision each time he looks away from his hands.

Fascinated by this description of lucid dreaming, I began to practice. I had, as many people do, had dreams before where I received a momentary flash of "this is just a dream," or "I'm only dreaming," so I assumed it must be possible to go farther than that.

The process took me several months. For some it takes longer, for some a much shorter period of time. I once told a class of high school students I was teaching about the Don Juan technique. One of the students walked into class the next day saying, "It works!"

"What works?" I asked, absorbed in something else.

"Looking at your hands," she explained patiently. "It works. I tried it last night and it worked fine until I got interested in something else in the dream and went off somewhere."

The values of lucid dreaming, in my opinion, are many. Awareness in the dream state can lead to an on-the-spot working out of personal problems, not to mention the pure fun and creativity possible. Since the subject of lucid dreaming is one infrequently discussed in dream literature, I will just record in this chapter a few examples of my own experiences with lucid dreaming as well as those of a friend, and go on to a discussion of some of their implications in later chapters.

On December 18, 1972, I recorded in my dream notebook:

> I heard a knock at the apartment door. There was
> no one there. It was dark in the apartment. I pushed on

the door. It came open, but from the hinge side. I thought, why I'm dreaming! I'm astrally projecting! Well, if you can do that, I said, then you can put your hand through this wall here. So I pushed on the wall. The wall opened and I stepped outside. It was dewy, warm, dark, and beautiful. I bounced up and down a couple of times, way off the ground. I traveled around a bit, but decided I'd had enough and "flotated" back into my own apartment again.

Then there was a sequence where I was changing my apartment. When I first came into it I thought it wasn't mine because the walls were covered with different types of fabrics, silks mostly, tiedyes with colors, brocades with prints. I took a piece of the ceiling, about pillow-case size and began changing its colors.

Then there were people in the room. There was a man who looked very familiar. I knew him, though I don't know him in real life. He grasped my hand and said something like, "So you finally made it." He was just on his way out (had his jacket on, one of those brown suede jackets with lamb's fur lining). He said, "Those people will want to talk to you."

I said, "I made it?"

"Yes," he said in a somewhat puzzled voice, "but you're very, well, earthbound. There are other places to go you know."

He acted as if he couldn't understand why I was so earthbound, but he repeated, "They'll want to talk to you," indicating the two women nearby, and moved as if to leave.

"Oh, I can explain why I'm earthbound," I told him, and the two women came over to hear. He was still holding my hand. We were old friends. "I used to do acid (take LSD)," I explained, "and this dream was a lot like doing acid, but when I went further, I always felt like I had John with me. Now, I'm afraid of what I might meet alone."

"But don't you think those things might be figments of your imagination?" he said.

"I'm sure they *are* figments of my imagination," I replied, "but...."

Well, before I even had a chance to talk to the two women, there I was in the same sequence again. I was in bed. There was a sound at the door. It sounded like someone was coming in. I got up. No one was there. It was dark, but there I was in the living room again. This time it was like there were shadowy forms behind me, reaching out long, shadowy arms. I thought about Ann Faraday's statement about turning to face the dream

reality as a way to vanquish it.
    I turned, but the forms remained behind me. I whirled. "You'll have to do better than that," I said. I was laughing and turning but I was also afraid. Every time I turned, the shadow was still behind me. I whirled into the bedroom and came near the long mirror, but it was dark and I was terrified of what I'd see. "This time I'm going to wake up," I said, and the next thing I knew I was waking up. I made myself sit up in bed so I wouldn't go on dreaming.

The question of the shadow or the type of shadowy form observed in this dream is often discussed in classic dream literature, discussed by Jung by just this name—the shadow. In traditional dream interpretation the shadow represents the shadowy parts of the unconscious or subconscious, and in my own dreams it seemed to represent just that.

As a matter of fact, in addition to being a major event in my lucid dreaming, this dream of grappling with shadowy forms uncovered one of my major underlying fears, and this shadow reappeared from time to time until that fear was dealt with.

As stated in the last line from my dream notebook, after the encounter that night with the dream shadow, I was so terrified that I made myself sit up in bed with the light on so I wouldn't go on dreaming. This was about 3:30 a.m. Finally, after a couple of hours of writing, reading and drinking hot chocolate, I was exhausted to the point of going back to sleep. Almost immediately I found myself in a room full of people telling them about the dream I had just had. Then some of these same people were driving me up to the gates of a formidable stone building, obviously an insane asylum. I was screaming and protesting that I wouldn't go. Later in the dream I found myself strolling down a flower-bordered sidewalk saying, "It's summer already. I must have been here a long time."

The lucid dream dredged up what I discovered to be long-repressed fears that my awareness of other than ordinary reality would result in incarceration. In the next weeks I recalled scenes from my childhood where I, the youngest of the family, was taunted by my then teenage brothers with, "They'll send you to the looney bin," and "It's Travers City (the area mental institution) for you." This type of teasing is, I'm sure, common to most children and, unfortunately, like most very young children I obviously believed it and curtailed my "abnormal" behavior.

Not accustomed to nightmares or even to dreams that were particularly frightening, I experienced during this period of conflict between my growing dream awareness and my repressed fear of being crazy, a series of dreams in which the shadow returned. Finally in one dream over a year later the shadow appeared behind my bed, slightly out of my line of vision over my left shoulder. I grabbed the shadowy form with both my hands and grappled with it. Though it seemed stretchy and somewhat elastic, I grabbed one of its formless arms and flung it with all my might across my body and over my right shoulder. The dreams ceased.

All of my dreams were not fearful by any means. All that winter I practiced with lucid dreaming, practicing various methods to learn how to control it.

One morning, waking up early and making the note, "It's too early to see the time yet," I recorded this dream:

> Suddenly realized I was dreaming and looked at my hands. I was in a bedroom/sitting room somewhere. Looked at my hands, looked away. It was decorated in rose pink. Looked at my hands, then at a panel of wooden closet door, thinking how Don Juan said to stabilize a few objects at first—but I was so curious I finally decided to go ahead and look at the room.
>
> It had a cushioned wooden seat to the left of me, a rug with a floral design on the floor. The walls had a pink brocaded look. A fireplace was straight ahead of me. There were several things on the mantel, including little carvings. One carving of a donkey caught my eye because it reminded me of the onyx elephant I had just bought (in waking life). There were some letters, and somehow I decided to tear out a stamp to remind me where I was. (I was still worrying about losing contact with my consciousness.) I tore out a stamp with a brownish background, a small design, some foreign printing, but the words I recall are Republique d'Egypt.
>
> Then I was in the next room, a bedroom, with a boy and two girls, college age perhaps. I was most aware of the boy. It was as if they had been conjuring up spirits because one of the girls seemed to be quite afraid. The boy was telling her, "Well, speak" (implying now we've got her here, say something to her).
>
> I laughed and said to the boy, "But you see, I'm dreaming you." He wouldn't believe me. The boy had dark hair, olive skin, an aquiline nose. The girl who was afraid had dark, short, styled hair and wore slacks. These two were reclining on the bed. The second girl, whom I don't remember exactly, was sitting at the foot of the bed. I was at the head of the bed near the boy.

Then I woke up in the dream. I put my hand in my pocket and pulled out the stamp to prove to myself I had been there.

I then awoke in "reality" in my bed. It was before daylight—maybe 5 a.m.

My friend Henry was very against the idea of lucid dreaming, arguing that the lucid dream implied attempts to control the dream reality (which of course it does), and that such control would stultify the natural ability of the dreamer to dream helpful and important dreams. He argued that dreams should be left alone and we frequently found ourselves in friendly combat, I saying that he should try lucid dreaming and he arguing that I should give it up.

One day I was to receive a visit from my former husband and Henry, like an old family uncle, was worried about me. Would I be o.k.? Did I want him to stay around? Would I call him if I needed him? I reassured him as best I could that I would be fine.

That night I awoke to find Henry sitting in a chair by the windows in my living room. I realized that I was dreaming, sat up from the couch where I was sleeping, and chuckled. I went to the chair where he sat.

"You're dreaming, Henry." He looked at me disbelieving. I sat on the arm of the chair and put my fist through one side of it and out the other. Then I bounded up and did a few free flight steps in mid air. "Will you remember this?" I asked.

"No," he said.

The next morning Henry came to my house wearing the most sheepish grin I have ever seen. "Do you remember what happened last night?" I asked him.

He shook his head no.

Was it all my imagination? I could more easily believe that, had I not had other experiences such as a more recent dream in which I was aware of a friend's being in trouble with some rather cataclysmic event such as a fire. I went to help.

The next day I asked her, "Do you remember the dream we had last night?"

She visibly paled and sat down. "Oh my God," she said, and called to her husband. The story came out that he had been having a rather violent dream involving a fire the night before and had awakened her by thrashing about in the bed. He described the dream to her and they both went back to sleep, whereupon she began to experience the same dream sequence, and this time she woke him up. She recalled my being there in the dream and said to him before they both went back to sleep, "You watch. Jean will

19

remember this dream."

In the early days of my lucid dreaming I spent a great deal of time experimenting with the possibilities of the dream state ranging from the very fluid and sometimes chaotic state of what I considered to be ordinary dream state to the fairly solid and unchanging world of what I considered to be the ordinary waking state. I had by this time read the British author Oliver Fox's classic book *Astral Projection* as well as the lesser known work of a contemporary American experimenter, Robert Monroe's *Journeys Out of the Body*. I realized there were and had been other people who had experiences comparable to mine called out-of-body experiences or OBEs, sometimes from the sleep state and sometimes from a full waking state. There were certain experiences they described that I wanted to experiment with.

One of these was seeing my physical body while being "outside" of it. The books discuss such things as roaring sounds and/or pain while "exiting" from the body at one point or another such as the solar plexus or the top of the head; and the fright of looking back to discover one's body sleeping on the bed or couch while the consciousness or "astral body" is hovering above or somewhere outside it. I must admit I have never had these experiences, though they seem to be quite common. And, quite frankly, it was this that made me begin to question such traditional metaphysical concepts as the astral body and the out-of-body experience. Metaphysics is by its proper definition the study of the physical which goes beyond our current understanding of the physical, thus allowing a certain amount of conjecture or theorizing; but if the currently accepted Einsteinian physics is true, it already places definitions on time, space, and matter which allow for their flexibility. What was to say that our present definition of the body was not equally limited by Newtonian physics without having to invent such devices as astral bodies or traveling out of the body? Further, I reasoned, if it is true that reading Jung or Freud or other dream analysts tends to produce Jungian or Freudian or other similar dream symbols in the dreamer, what would stop the person who had read certain metaphysicians from similarly creating symbols of astral bodies or other bodies?

For me, it was much more a matter of trying to determine whether or not I was asleep and then deciding what to do about it. Three dream experiences I had during this early period of lucid dreaming, for example, were like these:

> January 8, 1974:
> Waking up in bed, put my hand through the bed clothes, (For some reason I early determined that, as a

signal, if I could put my hand *through* the bed cover I must be asleep. This is a signal I still use) looking at my dream hand, shadowy in the light of the full moon. Put my hand down into the mattress making excited noises, feeling free and crazy—thinking, "Well, if this is what it's like to be crazy!"

Upon waking kept half-waking and half-sleeping. I wanted to go back to the state where I could project, but wanted to be aware of it. Caught myself a couple of times rising or falling.

January 25, 1974:

Afternoon. I dreamed I was in a development where gutters were dug but no construction yet was going on. It was raining. I began to climb up a hill, following the guttering. Suddenly I began to slide back down the hill. Realizing I was enjoying the fall, I became aware that I must be dreaming.

Then I was in bed looking at my hands, saying, "Hands, hands, hands, hands." I had trouble bringing them into focus.

February 5, 1974:

I "woke" and stuck up my hands to look at them. Realizing my hands were free, I simply pulled out of my body, swung my legs over the side of the bed and got up. I remember looking back at the bed to determine if I could see my body. I was a little worried that the fright of seeing my own body would wake me up—no body on the bed.

I went through the door from the bedroom. I distinctly remember the feeling of going *through* the door as opposed to around it, as if the door sort of enveloped me for a minute. Then I went through the front door. It was harder to get through that and I had to concentrate to get myself out of it.

Outside, last night's snow had melted and it was warm. I'd been wondering if one got cold in the snow in an astral body.

Then, after a glide down the street, I lost track.

Being of a practical nature, I also spent a fair amount of this early lucid dreaming time trying to determine what I could do in the lucid dream state or the waking state.

On February 6, 1974, the day following the dream of going through the doors, part of the dream events I recorded were:

There was a place where I was in bed thinking what could be done with this thing of a practical nature (don't forget, I was asleep) and found I could easily get the candlestick to move off the bedside table by just thinking about it, but then I realized it was only happening in that reality and not waking reality.

By April 10th I recorded:

Last night was another one of those—I was cold all night and realized I should turn up the electric blanket, plus I'd gotten to bed late and was worried about waking up in time for work, but flit, flit, flit. I wish I could determine the purpose of these dreams *consciously*.

I think the first thing I did in the dream was reach out of the sheet to turn up the electric blanket. I realized I wasn't "awake" and would have to wake up to do so. But I got hooked into "getting up."

In the living room I found that the fireplace and the stove were in the corner where the table sits. By thinking, I moved the fireplace back into place.

Back in the bedroom my bike was by the dresser (I kept my bicycle in the apartment to avoid theft). I pushed it, then realized it was a bike in addition to my own bike which was where it should have been. I found myself saying, "Two bikes, four bikes, six bikes . . ." as the bikes multiplied.

Getting back into bed, I realized I had intended the next time I was conscious like this to ask for spirit aid or at least try to see someone to talk to about this whole thing. I began asking and found myself moving up and out of the apartment windows, up into the air for what seemed like a long way. I remember myself thinking, you've got to remember this, but fearing I would not.

Later that same month I again found my bike in the wrong corner of the room during the dream state and directed it, by thinking, to "get back in place." It did, but it came apart as it did so and then I spent time trying to reassemble it by giving mental directions.

All lucid dreamers, like non-lucid dreamers, do not dream alike, though the major component of being aware of dreaming while the dream is happening remains the same. In order to give you a better picture of lucid dreaming I have included a series of dreams recorded by a friend of mine, Ed Ratcliffe, during 1977-78, during which he gained control of his lucid dreaming ability. Like many lucid dreamers, Ed found that breaking the sleep pattern with a nap during the daytime increased his lucid dreaming ability.

June 1, 1977—Alligator Dream

I had an incredible shamanistic type experience. I was in this house with my cousin Robert. I knew we were going through some kind of intense experience. In this room was a large bed which was at times a pool. At one point there was a tree beside it. On it was a painted alligator that I knew we had to bring to life. I beat on it many times and many ways with a stick. Finally it raised out of the wood. I knew this was my animal. Robert's was a huge black snake. The alligator suddenly, smoothly sank into the pool. I felt confident that I could hold his jaws open with my hands. He opened and I did. Then my grip gave out and in an instant my arm was snapped off. I was in sort of a state of shock but also coincidentally knew I was dreaming. Then almost as quickly my midsection was crushed in his jaws and I knew I was dead. There seemed to be a long pause, maybe other material I did not remember. Then I awoke in the dream with Robert on the bed. The bed had a hard metal frame. There was blood all around and especially a pool that poured through a hole in the bed to the floor. The hole had been made by Robert's erect penis at one point. I felt as I awoke here that I had been through this death in order to know that I could return to life in this reality. I felt an almost superhuman strength because of this knowledge. The intensity and feeling of this and the following part are really indescribable.

Then I was with my mother. We were sort of around the same place. I knew that because she had chosen to be with me that she would have to experience something similar to what I did. I felt afraid for her, not knowing if she could do it. There was an incredible wind throughout this, sometimes shaking the entire house. At one point a man, maybe like our former black maid, Susie, pulled a combine out of the house and headed out toward the field to cut the grass. The ominous feeling just hung for a long time. Then we decided to go somewhere and to my surprise I lost all memory of the ensuing trip. I felt I must have been so focused inside myself that I just missed it.

January 18, 1978—Star-Egg Dream (Nap)

I was here in the house at night. I noticed flashlights coming toward the porch. I went out and at first was blinded by the lights and could not figure out who it was. Then I figured it was our neighbors Jerry and Joyce or someone similar and with them was a young woman and her boy and girl children. I figured out that it was either Libby or a similar sister of hers. This was never too clear. We talked for a bit and they did not come in. I then went in and talked to John about it. I suggested he might want to invite them over sometime, but he seemed to decline which was all right with me since the two children had been pretty wild.

I then looked out the library window and saw a very bright moon high up in the sky. I noticed a second, dimmer moon near the horizon. This amazed me and I called John over to see it. He did not make it out right away and before he did, the top moon broke apart into four bright stars that seemed to crash behind the hill. John now arrived and I suggested we go talk to the people in the old house whom I figured had seen all this. As I talked we then saw three or so lights sort of rise up slowly like bubbles above the hill. This was then followed by an incredibly beautiful, nebula-like, ethereal blue and purple egg shape with one bright star inside of it and several dimmer ones inside and out. It moved slowly up and off.

NOTE: This dream has become a great evoking symbol for my dream exploration. The moon high in the sky is my waking, physical self which breaks into the four stars and descends behind the hill into unconsciousness, then to be reborn as the star-egg and the three stars rising into a dream sky. I did a collage of this dream and am still moved by it

2/1/78—Blue Body Dream (Nap)

Chris was here with a new girlfriend of his. I think she was part of a singing duo who had been together for many years. There was a lot of interaction here in the living room. She and Chris rubbed and touched each other a lot. She struck me as a little funny, kind of crazy and I wondered what had happened between Chris and Jeanne, who I knew had been together for many years. There was something that happened in the kitchen with folds of cloth or such and she sort of refused to clean it up feeling it was not her responsibility.

Then after some other action I became aware that I was lying on my back and there was a body suspended about two feet above me. It was light blue in color. I sort of visually caressed the body's side near the abdomen. I was aware simultaneously of my hand stroking the side of another more human body. I then realized, "Aha, this is a dream state." I then focused very sharply on the blue body's side. What I was seeing was very much like the images I get in a half-sleep state, but here they were sustained as I watched the body. It was like observing another reality rather than an imaginal world.

Now I thought to look at my hands. I tried to focus intently on the side to observe my hand caressing it. I was aware of a shadowy movement but did not get a clear image of the hand. Then in some way the belly of the body was touched by me and I saw it sort of ripple. The belly sort of hung down in a cone shape and came to a soft point at the belly button. All this time I was also aware of caressing a real body somewhere. The complexity of these two awarenesses eventually led to my losing consciousness. I drifted into ordinary dreams.

4/25/78—Navarro Dream (Nap)

I was in a large banquet hall or sometimes library stacks with many other people. Through some unusual circumstances I met a small man whose name was David Navarro. He had dark hair and a dark mustache and was only four and one-half to five feet tall. There were many interactions with him and others and then I stepped into one of the aisles and he was there with a tall, clean-cut blond fellow. David looked at me pointedly and asked if I recognized this fellow. I stared closely at him but couldn't quite place him. Navarro then showed me some photographs of this fellow in which he contorted his face in many shapes. Soon thereafter in a scene connected with a college friend, I had an incredible realization that the blond fellow was merely one of Navarro's transformations and it was a tremendous act of power for him to appear as both to me. I was awed by this.

Then I was driving through a strange town with Pat and John and some others. I needed some gas and knew there was a station up ahead. The town had one stoplight. We stopped at the Jewish synagogue and started in. As I expected, Navarro was standing out front, only here he was a massively built older black man with several companions. They were talking and he was doing some figuring on a calculator. I pointed him out to those I was with as we went into the synagogue.

8/4/78—I Look At My Body

I was sleeping here at the house and Mother seemed to be sleeping here also. Our next-door neighbor, Pat, turned his stereo on very loud with some screechy rock and roll, maybe Led Zeppelin. This woke me and Mother both up. I was not in my usual room but in an upstairs room that was my room. Soon the music stopped and Pat came over to use the bathroom and get ready for work. He was very down and upset that nobody appreciated his music. He said that Paul Mays had always been able to talk to him, but that nobody that he now knew could. He wanted new friends. I tried to talk to him but couldn't then. So he went on and I went to the bathroom. I was standing looking in the bathroom mirror and noticed my eyes were very red and swollen and thought at first that this was due to being awakened

at such an hour. But then I said, "No, this is a dream."
There was a moment of question as I felt my arms and
tried to feel if anything was unusual. So I looked back
into the mirror and my eyes were normal which kind of
confirmed it was a dream to me. Then I decided if this
was a dream I could go look at my body. I went into the
room and looked at the bed which seemed to have a
body completely covered over the head by a white cover.
I walked over and threw off the cover. There underneath
was my body sleeping. I moved at the surprise but did
not awaken. I had on some type of red garment. When I
moved on the bed, the me watching felt the movement
some way, as if it were a vague memory. I reached down
and touched my face feeling the roughness of my beard
and such. It definitely looked and felt like my body.

Eventually I went into one of the other upstairs
bedrooms where there were several older men and women friends. I told them all that this was a dream and
that they could see their bodies. Some were skeptical
but several did and were relating to these doubles of
themselves. It was all very loose and happy. I thought
how great it would be for this group of us to share more
dreaming in the future.

Then it was time for dinner and we started downstairs. I was next to someone and I said, "Why don't we
fly?" So I put my foot out and lifted off. We flew around
the living room for a time at about ceiling height and
eventually went into the dining room. After dinner I
was back in the living room with my sister Mary, who
was nude. We were ballet dancing together and I suggested we do it flying. It was very sensual and free as we
did. She was a little frightened by it at first. Eventually
we ran into some things and I commented that it was
good we were not on the ground because we might hurt
ourselves.

Then the workshop was breaking up and people
started leaving. They seemed reticent to formally say
good-by to me and just left. This then went into a long
series of dreams with an odd quality to them like a
remembrance of lucidity. I was at one point in this coal
town in the mountains. I asked about some tin cabinets
that were there by the tracks. One was huge and a young
woman said, "You couldn't carry that home in a truck."
There was a whole deep mine section there, very heavy
and mysterious. I met one of the workshop people there
who spoke briefly. There were other people, actions and
intrigues.

I was finally driving down a rain-soaked hill at
night with very little brakes. I passed this cartoon dog

running across the road. This reminded me that this
was a lucid dream. I then came into New York City with
many lights. This then flowed into my driving through
the aisles of a fast food place. Some girl said that I
couldn't drive through there if it weren't for the fact that
I was headed for Bluefield and this was the only way
through. I told her I knew that. I stopped at a phone
booth and spent some time dialing Mother's number in
Beckley. I awoke.

   I felt disoriented upon awakening and for a time
could not figure where I was sleeping. I finally figured
this out and spent a while replaying the dream in my
head until finally thoughts seemed to rush into my head
and I realized I had not been talking to myself since I
awoke.

Up to this point in his dreaming experiments, Ed was simply
learning how to lucid dream, but on March 16, 1978 he wrote, "I
would like to present, sort of out of context the dream experiences I
have had recently. I had been suggesting to myself for a while, 'I am
conscious in my dreams.' I had had two lucid dreams in the last
month, the first strongly lucid experiences I have had. I have for a
time been sleeping a two- to three-hour nap period in the afternoon
while reducing the number of hours I sleep at night. All of my
lucid experiences so far have come in this nap period. In addition I
have been taking some time recently to enter mildly altered states
and there explore my internal imagery. I have done this as an
attempt to enter an almost dream state from this side of reality.

   "One day, along with the suggestion above, I suggested that I
would meet some dream friends. I had the following experience:

   I was in the hallway of my house here. I felt like I
had been up and walking around for a while. I was sure
that I was fully awake. I looked out the door and saw a
man pull up to the house in a large black car. (This is
the first discrepancy, since the bridge to our house has
been out for some months. I still insisted I was awake.)
There were also two strange cars parked in our neighbor's driveway. There were puddles in the field by the
driveway and steam was rising from them. I figured this
man was a salesman. Since I did not want to deal with a
salesman right then, I walked into the utility room so he
would not see me. He walked up on the porch and
somehow I saw him there and realized he was very short,
three or four feet tall. As I waited he knocked and then as
easy as you please, he came in the door and started
walking in the house. I was angered by his nerve and
went in to stop him from coming in. He was now a

small form that was audaciously marching into the
room pulling a rope behind him that I thought had my
dog Murphy on it. I kept insisting I was awake as the
discrepancies grew. I was feeling panicky by now and
reachied down to grab him as he turned. When I touched him he was now the form of a cat made of soft ice
bubbles that steamed, just like the puddles outside. I
grabbed this cat form by the neck and threw him out the
door with the rope trailing behind. I followed him out
on the porch and now saw Murphy running around in
the yard. I then saw an exact copy of Murphy trotting
down the hill toward me. I started to move toward him
when a huge wall of water swept down the contour of
the hill into the field. I slowly came awake.

Ed comments, "Both suggestions were followed in this dream.
My insisting throughout that I was awake is my way of saying I am
conscious in my dreams. The salesman was apparently my dream
friend Navarro with something to sell. I certainly gave him one
hell of a welcome. As I am sure I am awake, my dream throws up
event after event to jar me out of that thinking. I never make the
leap to the fact that this is not my normal waking life.

"This experience reminded me of several that Carlos had with
Don Juan and especially one that Pablito had with the Nagual in
the form of a basket, from *Tales of Power*. Pablito's panic is
analagous to mine in that he believes he is awake and firmly in his
physical reality, and the Nagual shows him in incredibly wild
ways that no, he is not firmly set in physical reality, that he is in a
much more wondrous reality that he needs to become aware of.

"After this experience I decided to change my suggestion to, 'I
know when I'm dreaming.' The next afternoon I used this suggestion and the one about meeting dream friends and had this
experience:

I was standing in the hallway looking out the door.
I felt very much awake. I saw a large bird in a tree above
the road. He was like a hawk, but I realized his propor-
tions were like those of a sparrow and he was the size of a
turkey. I reached over and picked up the binoculars that
were lying there. It took me a moment to focus them and
I thought my friend, John, who has a different eyesight
from mine must have used them. The bird then flew and
I followed him with my binoculars. He didn't flap his
wings though. He just moved around in the air in his
normal standing position. I then realized the discrepancy and said, 'This is a dream.' It was difficult to say
that because everything still seemed so real. When I said
this I was then aware of lying on the bed physically

almost awake. I didn't move and very soon fell back to sleep. Then I was walking up the road below where I had seen the bird earlier. I felt as if during the time I almost physically awoke I had simply walked out the door and started down the road. I just picked up this dream state where it came in naturally.

I was very much aware as I walked along that this was a dream state though I had to remind myself of this occasionally. I walked along feeling the gravel beneath my feet. The sound of the stream rushing was very strong. I stooped down and as I did I felt a pain in my knee which had bothered me earlier in the day. I scooped up some water from a mud puddle and tasted a bit, feeling the grit in my teeth. All appeared perfectly real. Occasionally a discrepant event would occur and sometimes I would fall into a brief dream and sometimes I would become aware of my body on the bed as the cat that was actually sleeping next to me moved or I felt an itch somewhere.

The experience seemed to last a little longer than an actual trip down the road would take. I reached the end of the road and found a television set in a tree. I turned it on and watched. There was a woman on the screen and I thought, "Well if this is a dream I should be able to feel her body." I touched the screen, it had bumps and curves in all the correct places. I watched for a bit and then drifted into dreams and soon came physically awake. I decided not to pursue it further this sleep period and awoke to write my experience.

Ed interpreted the dream as follows: "Again my suggestions were followed in the dream. I knew I was dreaming and I assume the bird was my dream friend. The sparrow is most likely a reference to Scott Sparrow, who flies without moving his wings.

"My thinking processes in this state are very different from my usual thinking processes. I did not entertain any of the ideas I have thought about in waking reality of what I would like to do in a lucid dream. I was completely involved in that state, though I still felt the connection with my self on the bed.

"My perceptions were crystal clear and heightened. The touch of the TV screen reminded me of sensations I had had in LSD experiences. I took a walk down the road after I awoke in order to experience the sensations from a physical perspective. I realized that the perceptions I remembered from the dream state were actually stronger than those I was experiencing immediately in the world around me. In fact those remembered perceptions seemed to heighten my awareness of physical reality.

"And one other thought. When I awoke to write down my experiences, I reached over to put the phone on the hook. It accidentally fell off which surprised me. I then thought, 'What if a discrepant event should happen in my waking state? Would I then believe I was dreaming?' This thought moved and shook me."

This sampling of lucid dreaming experiences should give some idea of what the process might be like. In talking, by now, to literally hundreds of people about their dreams, I have discovered that this sort of dreaming is not at all uncommon though many people do not have lucid dreams with the frequency of mine and Ed's; nor do they apparently always talk about them. Some people feel they will be thought of as strange for talking about such experiences and others, I find, simply think this is the ordinary state of events and therefore there is no reason to talk about it.

Yet certainly it can be said that there are certain things common to lucid dreaming which are not ordinary to the dreams generally discussed in the literature of dream interpretation.

1. The dreamer is "awake" at some level, and realizes that a dream is in progress.

2. It is possible to a small or large extent to control what is happening in this state depending, I think, on first giving credence to it and secondly on practice. In my case, as in the case of many people, the lucid awareness is frequently mixed with periods of more ordinary dream reality in which I am not conscious of dreaming.

3. In the lucid dream state, actions tends to follow much more closely upon the emotions or feelings of the dreamer. That is to say, if I think of someone or some place I am almost immediately there and if I feel some particular emotion such as fear or joy, the events in the dream world immediately reflect it. This is true, of course, of the un-lucid dream state as well though in that case there does not seem to be such awareness of cause and effect.

4. In the lucid dream state, the laws of physical reality do not seem to be in effect, such as the law of gravity. It is possible to fly, to levitate objects, and to make things happen by simply thinking about them. Almost everyone who has ever recalled a dream has recalled a dream of flying; and though some people use their arms like wings, and others make motions of swimming in air, while others just lie back and let it happen, all recount the same feelings of freedom and joyful expansion. It is my belief that these flying dreams and the lucid dream state are very closely connected.

5. The dreamer may have some feeling of displacement, of being in two places at once. This is called by some, astral projec-

tion, as I said earlier; and some believe that the spirit or astral body actually leaves the physical body, connecting the two by an etheric cord which can be seen in this state as well as either or both of the bodies. For some there is a physical feeling of pain on what is thought to be exiting or re-entering the body and many people report loud noises or roaring sounds or feelings of rising or falling which are quite upsetting, such as a feeling of rapid descent back into the body just prior to waking.

6. Sometimes it is difficult to tell just which state has been achieved and whether one is awake or asleep. The dreamer often thinks he is awake only to find he is still dreaming. This is called in dream literature "false awakening," and several of the dreams recorded in this chapter demonstrate what I mean.

I once had a student, a young college girl who, until she became involved with people who were receptive to dream discussion, said she had not recalled any dreams in years. She determined to use the dream state to work on a particular problem which had been bothering her, bought a dream notebook, and gave herself the suggestion before going to sleep one night that she would remember her dreams long enough to write them down.

In the morning she woke with the following dream sequence, revolving around the problem she had set out to solve. She had a dream, awoke in the dream state and wrote it down; returned to "sleep" and had another dream and "awoke" to tell the dream to her roommates; returned to "sleep" had another dream and awoke in ordinary reality to write the dream down.

When she began to record the third and final dream in her dream notebook, she remembered that she had dreamed the other two dreams and also recorded them, feeling the whole time that she had done this already. She claimed later that she certainly had gotten more than she bargained for.

Chapter Three

What, Then, Is A Dream?

Obviously by the time I got to the point of lucid dreaming, I had some serious questions about just what a dream was. I had read many books on the subject of dreaming and still found huge gaps where the answer should be to the question of what is a dream.

Contemporary dream research, as it is carried out in dream laboratories across the country, has determined many things about the nature of dreams. It has determined that individuals generally dream in particular patterns throughout any sleep period and that these patterns generally occur in a reliable manner. The "normal" individual's sleep pattern can be recorded by an Electroencephalagraph (EEG) machine on a graph which resembles mountain peaks and valleys. And these peaks and valleys picture the sleeper's breathing patterns, heart patterns, mind wave patterns, etc., as he goes into the deepest levels of sleep and returns four or five times during any ordinary night.

Sometime around the middle of one of these peaks or valleys (depending on how you want to look at it) there occurs a period of time called by the dream researchers REM or rapid eye movement time during which the sleeper's eyes move, eyelids flutter, and if the sleeper is awakened during this interval, generally a dream is recalled as having been in progresss. These REM periods generally occur every sixty to ninety minutes and last for increasingly longer times, the longest lasting approximately thirty minutes.

Dream researchers have also determined that the dreamer's environment may or may not have something to do with the dream recalled; i.e., an arm falling to the side of the dreamer's couch may induce a dream of falling; ice may induce a dream of extreme cold, etc.; but not significantly enough to conclusively prove that dreams result from "something you et."

They have determined that a larger number of women than men surveyed dream in color. Admittedly, this synopsis of dream research is very brief and by no means detailed, but what do dream researchers tell us about what a dream really *is?* Very little.

Part of the reason for this, of course, is that Western science knows relatively little about the human mind and how it works. In fact in some ways it could be said that we know little more about the sleeping mind today than did our ancient Greek counterparts thousands of years ago when Plato recorded Socrates, the gadfly of Athens, as saying in the dialogue, *The Phaedo,* "You know that if there were no alteration of sleeping and waking, the tale of the sleeping Zyndmion would in the end have no meaning because all other things would be asleep too and he would not be distinguishable from the rest."

We know more about neurological patterns, of course, and about the composition of the nerve cells and the brain cells, but how these work together to make a single thought, let alone a dream, is still a mystery.

There have been many theories propounded as to what a dream might be. Jung's theory of the collective unconscious and contemporary psychoanalytic theories which subdivide the mind into such categories as the conscious mind, the subconscious, the super-conscious, ego, id, affect, etc., are only the beginning of theories which say the dream comes from releasing the subconscious mind during sleep and so on. It might be noted here that most psychoanalysts leave the question of where dreams come from to scientists of other persuasions and tend to deal as a whole with the result instead, the practical use of the dream.

Thus I found, and I fear you will find unless you are much more fortunate or wiser than I, that after a vigorous reading of both light and weighty tomes on the subject of dreams by dream researchers, scientists and psychiatrists, I returned to the same fundamental questions:

What, exactly, is a dream? Were the parallels I drew between some dreams and some drug-induced states simply the delusions of a drug-warped mind? Was anything, "just a dream," and if so, what? What were the implications about time and space if it was possible to dream about a future event and then have the "dream come true" days or weeks later? Why did some people remember dreams all the time while others recalled them seldom or never? Why could some people determine that they would dream the solution to a particular problem and wake up with the answer fresh in their minds when they might have worked on the same problem for a long time in the waking state with no significant solution?

By 1971 I had begun to investigate the world of psychic phenomena, at least in part because it appeared to me that psychics were presented with the same problems as dream researchers. Why was it possible, for example, for the well-known American trance medium Edgar Cayce to enter a state which resembled sleep and come out with the answers to questions, answers he did not know while in the waking state, including discussions of the future and the far past? How was it possible for the British psychic Joan Grant to go to sleep and enter into what she called "far memory" or recollections of stories from what she called past lives? Was this just their "imagination," as it was just my imagination that certain unusual experiences could not be explained by the light of current scientific theories; or was there, in fact, something missing in the theories?

I became director of Poseidia Institute (then known as the Association for Documentation and Enlightenment) in 1976. The purpose of this institute is to develop a wholistic approach to healing which combines intuition with science. In the years between 1971 and the present I have met and known personally dozens of practicing psychics and read the work of dozens of others. It is here, I think, that exists the beginning of the answer to the question of what a dream is; and, though it may require some alteration of current scientific theories, my logic would not let me rest, and the inherent logic in the information given through this large number of psychics was what convinced me I was on the right track at last.

The logic is somewhat complex so I will go through it as carefully as I can. Do not be surprised if you do not understand it on the first reading. Few people do, but it is certainly worth going over again.

Let us return first to Socrates who, though he lived many thousands of years ago, was faced with much the same questions as we are today. When Socrates was a young man, a friend of his, Chaerophon, went to a famous psychic, the oracle of Delphi, and asked whether there was anyone wiser than his friend Socrates. The oracle replied, "No."

Socrates, a humble man, spent most of the rest of his life trying to determine whether there was indeed anyone wiser than he was; and, when he concluded that the oracle had been correct, addressed himself to teaching his wisdom to others, an act which resulted in his death.

In the rather complex arguments of *The Phaedo*, Socrates presents his belief that life and death must be a circle, that in order to have life, one must have lived before.

It is at least comforting to know that such theories about life before life, called by some reincarnation, and theories about the flexible nature of time and space which the Indian religions call *maya* or illusion, have in fact been popular from ancient times in most cultures of the world including our own American Indian cultures, though they have only recently achieved a degree of popularity in the Western world.

The nature of time and space is a subject which must give rise to questions from the dreamer, especially one who dreams about next week's events before they happen.

When Edgar Cayce was asked, while in the trance state, about dreams, he replied that nothing ever occurred in physical reality about which we had not previously dreamed. This, of course, leaves a lot of room for speculation. The theory developed by Cayce and other psychics such as author Jane Roberts, whose trance state books channeled by an entity named Seth are popular today, is that time and space as we perceived them are indeed illusions and that, in fact, everything, all time, all space, is happening at the present moment or, as the mystical religions put it, the eternal now.

The function of how any event can occur in what we see as time and space becomes a function of probability. Thus, when a psychic makes a prediction of the future, what is being predicted is what will occur if the energy of the present moment continues along the same vectors.

Psychic Ray Stanford of Texas explained this concept of time and space in a series of trance readings for the American physicist James Wray by making the following analogy: If you look at time as a Mobius strip, a strip of paper twisted to form a figure 8, you can consider that the point in the center is that point wherein all time converges. While viewed from anywhere else on the strip, it appears that time is linear in nature and that past, present and future exist as separate events.

If you consider the original Mobius strip as the individual and the individual's perception of time and space, then take an infinite number of these strips and connect them at the point of intersection which is the center of the 8. What emerges is a sphere wherein all individuals connect and can perceive individually or together a linear time line or (and this is the tricky part) also intersect at the center and can perceive time from the perspective of the present moment, or eternal now.*

In addition to resembling Jung's analogy of the collective

---

*Ray Stanford, *Journal of the Association for the Understanding of Man*, Vol. 3, No. 1, May, 1975.

unconscious, Stanford's analogy also is reminiscent of the old story of the blind men and the elephant where each of several blind men seizes a different portion of the anatomy of the elephant and describes the beast. Being individually much smaller than the elephant, they of course cannot describe correctly the entire animal.

If it *could* happen, however, what else might be true about the nature of time and space? Einsteinian physics presents us also with the theoretical probability that as mass reaches the acceleration of the speed of light, time becomes distorted as well, slows down to the point that the aging process stops or can even go backward in time—a theory which has given rise to an endless variety of science fiction tales of space travelers who return to earth as young men only to find new generations populating their homelands and young lovers left behind who have aged beyond recognition.

However, it is not all science fiction we are dealing with, and modern physics as a science has come closer than any of the other sciences to the "metaphysical" theories with which we are dealing here. As explained in the book *The Tao of Physics* by Fritzof Capra, and numerous other modern texts, the high energy physicist must deal with the mystery of particles which seem to appear and disappear at will in acceleration chambers, with the concept of the black hole, and the apparent reality of such things as matter and "anti-matter."

An appropriate illustration of the mysteries of time and space might be shown by a psychic reading which I witnessed being given in 1975 by Ellen Andrews-Negus at Poseidia Institute.

The reading was for a three and one-half-year-old boy who had been born with a large birth mark near his anus. Doctors had feared that there might be rectal damage but apparently there was none. However, at this age the child had never been toilet trained, suffered constant constipation, and cried whenever he had a bowel movement.

In addition he suffered from what were apparently allergies, broke out in hives and rashes, was terrified of fire, and was frightened of water and bathing.

He had been taken to numerous pediatricians who, again, could find nothing physically wrong with him, with the result that he became terrified whenever he entered a doctor's office. The worried parents came, as many people do, to a psychic as a last chance.

After some preliminary conversation, the parents went with the psychic into the room in which the reading would be given. The child, crying and trembling, was taken by a friend into another room.

When the psychic went into trance, the first thing to come out of her mouth were some of the most hair-raising screams I have ever heard in my life along with moans and the almost unintelligible words, "Help me, help me." The atmosphere in the room was electrifying.

The conductor (the person who conducts the psychic into the trance state, asks questions, etc.) demanded to know who was speaking.

After a few minutes more of cries and moans and reassurances from the conductor, it developed that the speaker was a Royal Air Force Captain whose plane had gone down over Scotland during World War II. The plane had burst into flames and the captain and all his crew had died in the fire, and in the water into which the plane fell. This captain, feeling grave responsiblity for his dying men, had obviously been traumatized by the situation.

After explaining that the time was now over thirty years later, and informing him of his quite obvious death in the tragedy, Ellen Andrews-Negus' conductor bade the entity be gone and the psychic continued with the reading. The time was 8:40 p.m.

The friend who was with the child reported that at that moment in another part of the building, separated by three closed doors, the boy put his hand on his back, said, "What was that," and soon after comfortably fell asleep.

The reading then given for the child stated that he had been in a previous incarnation a crew member of the plane which had gone down. The man whom the child was had been badly burned on his legs and torso. In addition, he had been traumatized by the attentions of his captain "from another area of time and space." The parents were given instructions for suggestions to be repeated to the child before he fell asleep as well as suggestions for massage and dietary changes to relieve the body of the toxins built up in the system from an excess of fear and anxiety.

Within a few weeks the parents reported that the child had begun to have regular bowel movements, that his fear of fire and his anxiety over bathing had begun to diminish, and that the apparent allergies, rashes and hives were no longer present. Now, a few years later, he is apparently a completely normal, healthy, happy individual.

What happened? This reading by any standards is extraordinary. Most psychics do not communicate on any regular basis with the spirits of the dead, or supposed dead, such as this RAF captain; nor is the cause so dramatic, nor the cure. The reading is by no means, by itself, proof of anything. Yet it does serve to illustrate some working hypotheses. That:

1. Time and space are not as we perceive them; are not linear but all time and space may be present now.

2. It may be possible to exist in more than one "present

moment" at once.

3. It may be possible to perceive more than one "present moment" at once, and also to benefit from that perception.

If time and space are illusion, why don't we perceive it? is the automatic question to ask. Why aren't we aware of other existences, other places, now?

The answer to that question is puzzling perhaps, but I doubt that it is any more puzzling than the answer to why, throughout most of what is called the Dark Ages, or Medieval times, in Europe did citizens believe that in fact the earth was flat and if one sailed too far in the direction of the edges, there would first be the encounters with strange and horrible sea monsters; and if the sailor were not done in by them, there would be the inevitable, horrifying fall off the edge of the earth itself?

Why, in our own century, did people laugh at the Wright brothers and others who believed it was possible to fly in heavier-than-air crafts, and say that if God had intended man to fly, He would have given him wings?

Why until quite recently, was it laughable that invisible microorganisms, perceptible only under the magnifying lens of a microscope, could be the cause of illness; and that doctors themselves, operating under less than sterile conditions, could carry these "germs" to the detriment of their patients?

And why was it only in the last few decades that scientists, inventors, and engineers discovered (and are still discovering) the usefulness of waves and frequencies which we know to populate "space" even though we cannot see them or hear them unless they are manipulated or amplified; and even still are not sure how, ultimately, they are generated?

The answers to all of these questions deal with the matter of perception, and the matter of perception has always been left to the pioneers, the inventors, the explorers and the creative thinkers.

To the Medieval mind, it was unthinkable that what could be seen with the naked eye (that the earth, if one stood on a flat plain, was flat; or that the sea stretched only to a flat horizon) could not be true; and it was left to adventurers and explorers to explain the difference.

Scientists say even today that we, our bodies, are not as the human eye perceives them; that in fact the human body or that table over there, or the leaves on the trees, are made up of whirling atoms with constantly interacting components and spaces in between. What is seen by the human eye, is, in fact, an optical illusion, a comforting and familiar one, but an illusion nonetheless.

So the question then becomes one of not if time and space as we perceive them are illusion, why are we not aware of it; but if time and space are illusion is it perceivable, and who and how many people perceive it?

A look at the shelves of your local book store or the public library should give you an answer to that. Early in this century a man by the name of Charles Fort made a hobby and then a life work of collecting from newspapers and other sources tales of the unusual and the unexplainable. Several volumes of his work recount stories of objects dropping from out of "space" inexplicable—stones, frogs, human beings.

The number of books about ghosts, haunted houses, and people who have seen ghosts alone would fill a full shelf in most libraries; psychics, psychic phenomena, parapsychology experiments, another shelf.

One of the gravest arguments against the validity of such information is that so little of it has been done under laboratory conditions. It is not repeatable. Many psychics as a matter of fact, and some of the best-known psychics in the world, have been unable to operate within parapsychology laboratories. And yet, by sheer weight of the number of people who report and have reported incidents of time warp, *deja vu*, precognition, etc., and the sometimes well-known and respected people who have done so—Taylor Caldwell, Mark Twain, Carl Jung, Henry Ford, Abraham Lincoln, Thomas Edison—to name just a few, we must at least wonder, and give some credence to the possibility that our understanding of time and space may not be as complete as it might be.

Both in trance state and out of it, the reason many well-known psychics have given for the fact that the ordinary individual is so unaware of the illusory nature of time and space is this: the human mind, of which even the best neurologists and biophysicists know relatively little, is, at least in part, a well-trained screening mechanism. It has been known for some time that we in fact "remember" only a fraction of what we have perceived, learned, or been exposed to; and yet, like a gigantic computer memory bank, the human mind can and does store information, probably all information with which we have ever come into contact, and this information under certain circumstances like hypnosis, or stress, or some particular stimulus can be recalled.

Our minds, the psychics say, have been programmed to retain only so-called useful information while information which is "just your imagination," "just a dream," or otherwise trivial is disregarded as unimportant.

How many times, however, have you experienced the feeling, the hunch, the premonition that you should not do something or that if you do something there will be a certain result? Disregarding the feeling, you go ahead and do it anyway. Only when the predicted result occurs, when what you thought the future might hold comes true, do you say, "I had the feeling I shouldn't have done that." Yet how did you know, if you were not, at some level, aware of what the future might bring?

What we are talking about here is a comparison between what is called reason or logic and what is called intuition. There is much study being carried on today by psychologists and medical researchers which compares right brain and left brain functions. Very simplistically stated, the left brain is said to govern the right half of the body and also such functions as logic and reason while the right brain controls the left half of the body and such functions as intuition.

The process of intuition, say psychics such as Edgar Cayce and Betty White, (a contemporary of Cayce's whose author husband, Stuart Edward White, wrote a whole series of books about her beginning with *The Betty Book*), is a process that is available to all of us, and is actually inherent in humanity. The difference between the psychic and any other person is simply that the person we call psychic trains or utilizes this intuitve ability while most of us either don't develop it or ignore it.

The psychic trains and develops the ability to perceive events that are happening in other areas of the time/space continuum such as next year, next door, or "another lifetime." A trained psychic is as easily able to tune in to a person in another country as he or she is able to tune in to a person in the same room, as if there were no space intervening. Most of us ignore or disbelieve such information.

Constant training from childhood that this sort of event is to be feared, is not to be talked about, or is to be written off as "just your imagination," say the psychics, is the thing that keeps most of us from realizing that the construction of reality is quite different from the way we ordinarily perceive it.

Thoughts are things, or variations on this adage, adopted by those who follow the thoughts of Edgar Cayce, is the real kicker which follows logically from a belief that all of time and space are present now. And I recommend that if you are not yet familiar with this concept you hold onto your hat and fasten your seat belt for the ideas that follow. For they are sure to unsettle you. Jane Roberts calls this reality creation, and there is quite a nice book by her on the subject called *The Nature of Personal Reality* which you might like to read.

The question, if you happen to conclude that all events are happening now, is how do we determine what events to perceive in order to believe we have past, present and future?

According to psychics such as Edgar Cayce, Betty White, Jane Roberts and Ellen Andrews-Negus, all things, everything, has consciousness.

When you speak of "myself," are you thinking of just your body or, in fact, are you thinking of more—of your thoughts, your feelings, the person you were at age five, the person you were last week?

Already you have begun to perceive something which the psychics take for granted. *I* am more than my body. I have a body, but that is *not all* there is to it. I am a being with a consciousness which extends far beyond my body.

The fact is, say the psychics, we create our bodies as our most personal waking symbol. Our bodies, as the rest of what we call "reality," are our own creations. And this reality is created by the process we call thought.

Jane Roberts, who discusses this theory most thoroughly in her trance book, *Seth Speaks*, contends that all of the known and unknown universe is filled with as yet imperceptible (that is, beyond the range of mechanical measurement) units which she names "electro-magnetic energy units," which come together to form matter perceivable to human measurement dependent on thought and the intensity of feeling behind that thought.

Other psychics, in their channeled material, concur. Betty White, in the book *Across the Unknown* speaks of the variations in vibration or intensity as that which keeps us from perceiving other areas of reality equally as real as any we perceive.

Again these ideas are not new to the world even though they are new to Western science and most of the world we live in. The teachings of many so-called primitive societies correlate with these thoughts very thoroughly.

In the teachings of the American Indians of the Western Plains region, the medicine wheel was used to explain that: all things are equal on the medicine wheel—you, me, a tree, a rock, a bear, another person. We are all reflections, one of another, placed here to learn from one another.

According to the Medicine Wheel teachings, if you were to place four objects (or any other number of objects) in the center of a circle of people and ask them to describe what they saw, each person would see through the filter of his or her own experience. If the object in the center of the circle were, say a bear, the hunter might see a prize to be taken; the child a friendly, furry creature; another person might see something frightening; and a fourth, an object of no interest at all. Each person has something to learn about himself from the bear.

And this, say the psychics, is the essential truth about the world we perceive as "real"—an idea not so far removed from the fact that what we see is an optical illusion made up of atoms and molecules moving and interacting at various rates of speed, reflecting or absorbing light.

The true quality of what we perceive comes not from any quality inherent in the object we perceive itself, but in our thought, in our feeling, and our emotions.

Have you ever asked several people to describe what they see or hear? This phenomenon has been made into the childhood game called gossip or telephone which you may have played sometime when you were younger. And it is a common joke among policemen or others who investigate crises or emergenices that the perpetrator of a crime may, according to witnesses, turn out to be a short, tall, man/boy of medium height wearing a brown, black, gray suit or blue jacket and driving an American car of foreign make.

The fact is that depending on how we feel, on what we are doing, on our education and background and many other factors, we all perceive things quite differently (or in some cases quite similarly), and the theory we are dealing with here is that we are not just perceiving what is already there but are creating it, making it into something we call physical reality.

We have all experienced the phenomenon of time passing slowly or quickly, and have many expressions for such things like, "Doesn't time fly when you're having fun?" When we are doing something enjoyable and interesting, time does seem to fly or the hours go by very quickly. Yet, put in a position of doing something dull or boring, every minute can indeed seem like an hour.

We have also experienced the apparent expansion and contraction of space. In the jet age, the television age, we talk of a "shrinking world" of "global neighbors." And again, when one is dreading the arrival at a particular destination, the trip can seem to speed by while if the destination happens to be a long-lost friend or lover, the "miles seem to drag." Each of us has experienced what driving manuals call "road hypnosis" where whole miles are lost because our "mind was somewhere else."

And what is happening, the psychics say, is that in what we call the waking state, we are all hypnotized, we are all in trance, all the time. We hold the world together by the sheer weight of our beliefs and the reinforcement we get from others about our beliefs. We believe this is a house because we want to believe that it is a house and the beliefs of many others from the lumberman to the contractor to the architect go into reinforcing our belief that it is a house.

Those historical figures and those among us who practice and experience unordinary things such as walking on hot coals, being cured instantly of incurable disease, bending spoons with the power of thought, seeing ghosts, and other acts which have historically been called miracles, have accidentally happened into or trained themselves into waking from the trance we call waking life into another belief which admits such things are possible.

The ultimate statement being made here is that we, each of us, create our own reality, and that reality is a living symbol for our inner life—our thoughts, desires, fears and emotions.

What, Then, Is A Dream? If our waking world is as much of an illusion as we consider our dream world to be, if time and space are illusion, and we create our own reality, what then is what we have been calling a dream?

As I've said, there are literally hundreds of books which deal with alternative ways of perceiving, of seeing time and space, and many of them are excellent. This is just a personal synopsis of what I have read and learned, but the question of what is a dream remains to be answered.

When we enter the relaxed state we call sleep, the control, the filtering process which we ordinarily allow to our mind in the waking state is also relaxed. We no longer have to believe in what we call the natural laws, the law of gravity, the laws of cause and effect, the laws of time and space and the result is a form of reality creation we call dreaming.

But do dreams happen only when we're asleep? Dream laboratories have graphed the cycles of sleep and pinpointed "dreaming" to a period called REM time. Yet the study of biorhythms both in humans and in other species indicates that all of life follows certain cyclic patterns which go on day in and day out, year in and year out; that certainly animal species follow the rhythms of the tides and the rhythms of the season whether or not these species are in their natural habitat; and that, just as certainly each individual has his or her own biorhythmic or body rhythm cycles.

Mikey McCorkel Sycalik, the psychic who founded Poseidia Institute, speaks (in trance) of trance time as REM time.

Seth, through Jane Roberts, contends that, awake, or asleep, we follow the same patterns indicated by sleepers in the dream laboratories and that we follow a cycle of being more focused or less focused on what we call physical reality. Daydreaming fits into this pattern as does the statement, "I'm asleep on my feet."

Further, Seth contends, the reason that participants in so-called primitive or ancient civilizations were more in touch with the flexible nature of time and space is that they were/are more in touch with the natural rhythms of life, less regimented by clocks and other devices of time, and that even the sleep state in these societies is likely to be broken up by activities which meet the daily needs for food, shelter and safety. Thus it is not possible to develop the common Western ideas that day is for being awake and night is for being asleep; that what happens in the daytime is real and what happens at night or in sleep is unreal, unessential and "just your imagination."

In fact *The Seth Material* suggests that it would be beneficial to anyone's general health and well being to break up sleeping and waking times; to nap during the day and be awake and active part of the night.

Just as scientific tests have proven that the human animal seems to need sleep for survival, that persons who have participated in "sleep deprivation" experiments often suffer severe hallucinations and bodily trauma, the psychic answer seems to be that the healthiest person is the person who follows as closely as possibly the body's own natural rhythms.

This is not as hard as it sounds even in our time-conscious modern society, though it does take some determination and, again, a belief that it might be worthwhile. I tried Seth's sleep suggestion and found that within a very short period of time my dream recall had improved considerably, that I felt like I had more than one day in a day since I generally awoke refreshed after I got over my initial tendency toward grogginess and had repatterned myself, and that all of my activities seemed to take on increased life and vitality. It was only after adopting this broken sleep pattern that I began lucid dreaming.

Like most people I was working at an eight-hour-per-day job. I had a social life as well. What worked for me was to nap for a couple of hours just after I came home from work. I shortened my nighttime sleeping hours by an equal amount so that I was sleeping approximately five or six hours at night and two in the afternoon.

This pattern may not work for you but there probably is one that will. The average adult human being does not need more than eight hours of sleep in any twenty-four-hour period. In fact more sleep than that, especially when taken in an unbroken manner, may be harmful to one's health or may indicate serious physical or emotional problems!

It is said that the adult Thomas Edison seldom slept. What he did do, however, especially when he was working, was relax in a chair holding steel balls in his hand. When he had relaxed sufficiently for his arm to drop, the metal balls fell to the floor and woke him up. This is a sleep pattern I doubt you will want to adopt, but if you are seriously interested in pursuing the world of dreams I suggest that you try the suggestion of breaking the pattern of day and night, waking and sleeping.

A dream then, if we follow the logic of this chapter, is nothing more *or less* than the creation of another reality, a reality different from the one that we know when we are awake, but equally valid, equally useful, and equally enjoyable. We can be as creative when we are dreaming as when we are awake. We can learn as much. We can do just as many things.

There is just one caution to observe. Because, in the dream reality, the period between thought and thing, between the emotion and the manifestation of emotion is likely to be brief, it is not suggested that one should try to understand dreams or work with the dream reality unless one is ready to investigate, to know and understand the inner workings of the self. The person who is afraid of self-understanding can be made very uncomfortable with dreams.

Because the theories presented in this chapter are likely to be difficult if they are unfamiliar, let me again summarize them, starting from the point that time and space are illusion.

1. If it is true that time and space are illusion, and everything is happening at once, then we exist in more than one "present moment" at once.

2. Our minds have been trained to believe that what we ordinarily perceive is the only reality, so that even if we are slightly aware of other "present moments" we tend to pass them off as imaginary. A psychic is a person who by nature of training perceives other existing "present moments."

3. The vehicle for determining what "present moment" we will perceive as reality is our thought and the intensity of that thought. Each of us creates an individual reality and, as a group, humanity creates a group reality which most of us believe is the only reality there is.

4. In sleep, the mind, the training of belief, the filter of other realities, relaxes as does the physical body we have created. In sleep we are free to experience other "present moments," other realities without the usual fear that these realities are just imaginary, are crazy, stupid, or even unusual.

5. In this system physical reality becomes a symbol just as dream reality is and can be interpreted as meaningfully, as intensely as can the dream reality.

6. It is possible to break down the barrier between waking reality and dream reality.

Like any other theory, however, this theory about the nature and meaning of dreams in order to be valid or useful has to be provable and workable. As the result of my own experience, I believe that it is; and I feel that each of us, with a little work, sometimes hard work, can prove it to ourselves since, in a way, we are each a dream laboratory and investigation team all rolled up into one, the most complex machine or measuring device humanity has every created.

In order to support this theory, I would like to present just some of the dream experiences I, and the many other people I have met on the journey of dream exploration, have had.

Chapter Four

Is It ESP, Or Am I Crazy?

I said in the introduction to this book, that one of my earlier recollections was of my mother's dreaming that her brother had been captured by the Germans. The dream itself probably took place very close to the time Joe was actually wounded and captured. Yet my mother woke, she said, knowing for certain that they would be informed of the fact of his capture, as later they were.

How could she have known what was happening to her brother when she was asleep in the United States and he was fighting in France?

How could she have been certain that the family would hear of his capture even though the telegram would not arrive for days?

I must admit flatly that I have never yet experienced a precognitive dream of just this sort, which very explicitly points out what is happening somewhere else or will be happening sometime soon. Yet many, many people have.

Once in college I was invited to a friend's house for a short vacation. The friend told me that her sister-in-law had very strange dreams. So when I met the sister-in-law, I'll call her Francie, I was curious to hear about the dreams she had.

All her life, Francie said, she had known exactly when someone close to her was going to die because she always dreamed about it before it happened. The first time, when she was ten, she dreamed that her grandfather, who was then in the hospital, would die the next day. She told her parents about it after his death, but they believed that she had just imagined it.

However, it continued to happen until she herself became

firmly convinced that she was having dreams which clearly predicted future events.

The year before my visit, with her usual accuracy, Francie had dreamed that she received a phone call from her mother-in-law, my friend's mother, who was crying and saying hysterically that Bob, my friend's father, had just had a heart attack and that she should come quickly.

In the dream Francie went to the house. The ambulance came. Her father-in-law was taken to the hospital where he was pronounced dead on arrival. He had been fine until that time (in waking life as well as the dream) and had played eighteen holes of golf just the day before.

When the phone rang the next morning, Francie knew who it would be and was ready to go to her in-laws' house.

Fortunately for Francie she also dreamed when more pleasant events would happen and had accurately predicted the sex and circumstances surrounding the birth of her first child and had done the same with several relatives and friends.

At the time I first heard about Francie's dreams I found them interesting and believable, due to my mother's dream, but gave it no further thought until years later when my own dream study began. I was reminded of Francie, however, one day when I was conducting a dream workshop at the College of William and Mary in Williamsburg, Virginia. In that workshop there were not one, but two people who had experienced vivid precognitive dreams similar to Francie's.

One was a young college co-ed who had never paid much attention to dreams until a few months earlier when she dreamed she was watching her sister riding in a car which was being driven along a dark road. It was raining and very dark. The driver of the car apparently did not see the car coming toward him until it was too late. He swerved; the car went out of control. The girl's sister was thrown out of the automobile.

Our dreamer was awakened by the sound of the telephone. It was the emergency room of a nearby hospital calling to tell her that her sister had been in an accident. Since her parents lived in another state, she was the nearest relative.

Still half asleep when she reached the hospital, the girl asked the emergency room nurse what had happened and then proceeded to retell the events before the nurse had a chance to open her mouth. Needless to say both the girl and the nurse were shaken by the accuracy of her report.

The sister, having been thrown out of the car, was not badly injured even though the driver was killed.

The other precognitive dreamer at this same workshop was a

middle-aged woman, elegantly dressed. As soon as the younger girl began to tell her story of the dream about the accident, this woman's interest in the workshop started to pick up; and, before the girl had finished, she could barely keep herself from interrupting.

"I have dreams like that," she blurted out as soon as she politely could; and nothing would do but that she tell her story to the by-now fascinated listeners.

This woman, it appears, was another who quite regularly predicted the deaths of loved ones, and only a few weeks earlier she and her husband had heard that a close friend of theirs was seriously ill and hospitalized in another city.

Earlier that week, the woman said, she had dreamed she went to the friend's hospital room and went to his bedside. He was very weak and in a coma. She knew that he would die.

The next morning when the phone rang before she got out of bed, her husband answered it. He came into the bedroom and she said, "It's about David, isn't it? He's dead."

"They call me a witch," the woman said as she finished her story. "They all think I'm crazy."

She proceeded to tell of another recent dream she had had about some property the family owned in another country. The family employed an overseer, she said, to manage this property which was large and had several tenants. In the dream she had visited the overseer who was new and had been employed on recommendation from a friend. The new overseer in the dream was in the process of swindling her and her husband.

After much conversation her husband was finally convinced that they should travel to their estate. When they arrived there they discovered that the new overseer had in fact been swindling them.

"My husband doesn't like me to talk about my dreams though," the woman said. "He thinks I'm crazy and doesn't want other people talking about me."

What this lady mentioned is a fear common to many people who have precognitive dreams or other experiences by which they can foretell the future: that people will think they are crazy. The disturbing part of all this is that it is so close to the truth.

It seemed that as soon as I became the director of an organization which researches psychic experiences, every time I would go out in public and mention the fact of my employment someone would begin nervously to tell me of some extraordinary experience they had had. Almost always this conversation began with, "You're going to think I'm crazy, but....."

If only the number of people who have confided in *me* were crazy, not to mention the number of people who have not, we would be living in a very crazy society indeed.

Yet we must face the fact, I think, that our society as a whole fears the unknown, the unusual, the unexplained. We are not so far away from the witch-burning days of Salem that we are yet comfortable with people who speak freely of predicting the future or seeing what does not "exist." And I must wonder, given the number of people who *have* talked to me of their fears of being taunted by people who call them witches or spooky, how many others there are who have had similar experiences which as yet remain untold because of these fears.

Was this intelligent, obviously well-bred and well-to-do wife and mother crazy, as her husband sometimes worried? Or was she simply experiencing something which is quite common, though not often spoken of?

And what trouble had the fear of talking about her experiences caused for her?

This same woman told of yet another dream she had recalled recently. She had been talking with her son who was limping and on crutches about the difficulty he was having with his leg.

"But there's nothing wrong with my son," she said. "He has never had any problems with his legs even though he played football and other sports all the way through high school."

The real questions that were troubling her then came out. "Should I tell him about the dream?" she asked. And, "What if the dream should come true? Am I causing these things to happen?"

How many people, I wonder, who dream the unusual, the unspoken of, wonder if in fact they aren't partially or totally responsible for the event happening in "real" life?

Louisa Rhine, wife of the world-famous American parapsychologist J.B. Rhine, tells the story of a dream she once had about their young son. The family was vacationing and, absorbed in something else, she failed to notice that her son, then just a toddler, had gone too near the water. When she looked, the child, in his bright yellow sunsuit, was in the water. In the dream he drowned.

Though Mrs. Rhine did not appear to be a woman who regularly had precognitive dreams, the dream appeared to make her more watchful; and when, in waking life, the following event occurred, she was alert enough to act. Down by the water, Louisa Rhine said, she found herself absorbed in the same activity she had been involved with in the dream. Finally alert to the fact that she was doing what she had been doing in the dream, she looked up only to see her child in his yellow sunsuit heading for the water. She jumped up, ran to him and led him back to safety.

The explanation Mrs. Rhine gives for the difference between what happened in the dream and what happened in waking life is very close to our explanation that everything is happening at the same "time." In the dream, because she was not alert, the event carried itself to one probable conclusion. With the dream as a warning, however, in waking life the event carried itself to another, far more pleasant conclusion.

Did Mrs. Rhine cause the event to happen by dreaming about it? No, in fact she was able to avert what might have been a tragedy by recalling her dream.

Looked at in the light of the theory that everything is happening in the "present moment" this statement can also be given further explanation. Every possible, every probable result or outcome of any decision we might make or any action we might take exists somewhere in the "present moment" in the form of energy, not yet physical. In the dream state we create situations, examine possibilities and probabilities, some of which we choose in the waking state to make part of our physical reality.

Another example of this type of dream was told to me by a friend who said that he and his wife were about to go on a trip. The night before they left, he dreamed that his wife, who was not licensed to drive in that state, was driving their car. Just as they reached the crest of a hill, they were stopped by a policemen who was checking vehicle registrations. The policeman asked for his wife's license, looked and saw that she was improperly licensed and issued her a ticket.

When they left on their trip the next day, my friend said that he, remembering the dream, told his wife he'd better drive. Sure enough, driving along he recognized the road just as he was driving up a hill; and at the top of the hill was a policeman checking vehicle registrations. The policeman stopped them, asked for my friend's license which was proper for driving in the state, looked at it, and signalled him to drive on.

The dream had saved both time and expense on the trip.

Was it just an accident that the dream and the waking event resembled one another? My friend says that he doesn't have precognitive dreams very often, yet he definitely recognized the hill and knew before he reached the top that there would be a policeman just beyond the crest of it.

Let's return then to the woman in the workshop and her dream about her son and his leg.

First, there is the question of whether she causes the events she dreams about to happen. Surely it would worry someone to believe that he or she has some major part in a traumatic event which they dream of happening to another, particularly if that event were a disfiguring accident or even death. Yet look at just the dreams discussed here. In part of the dreams the corresponding waking event happened just as the dreamer dreamed it. In part of the dreams, the dreamer used the dream result as a clue to changing the outcome of the event in waking life. Two things seem apparent from these dreams. One is that it appears that there *is* something about time that is flexible enough so that people, even very ordinary people, can see into the future—or, perhaps it is easier to say at this point, if not the future, at least into some other segment of time. The second thing that seems apparent is that, even though a dream may give one the outline of an event to come, not only is the dreamer not causing the event to happen by dreaming about it, but having seen one possible outcome in the dream, can create another outcome in waking life.

The best explanation I can give of the fact that people so often recall precognitive dreams of death or other traumatic events, again relates to the theory that time is flexible and that *what becomes physical is determined by our thoughts.*

Death and trauma are certainly events which are surrounded by intense thought and feeling. Even accidental death, if it is true that everything is happening now and some part of our being is aware of it, would have to set off a great intensity of feeling. And, just as we are often aware of the feelings from someone to whom we are close even while we are awake, certainly in the more relaxed state of sleep we would be more likely to be aware of intense feelings from someone we care for.

The second question from the woman in the workshop was whether she should tell her son about her dream about his leg. She knew she risked being laughed at even though her son was sympathetic toward her feelings and aware of his mother's dreaming abilities, and she especially risked being told she was worrying unnecessarily and should put the whole thing out of her mind.

My answer to this question was that certainly, with her track record for accurate precognitive dreams, it would be wise to tell her son about the dream and suggest that he might be careful since, as we have seen in the dreams of Louisa Rhine and my friend who was going on vacation, not only is the dreamer not responsible for creating the events dreamed in a precognitive dream, but may in fact be able to alleviate the waking life situation by this foreknowledge.

The same question about telling someone about a dream was asked of me by a friend, Roland, who said that he could not remember ever having had a precognitive dream before, but that he had had a dream a few nights prior to our conversation which bothered him because of its feeling of reality. He had dreamed that his brother (of whom he could never remember dreaming before) and a friend were going to go somewhere on their motorcycles. In the dream, the brother had hit a particularly uneven piece of ground and the motorcycle had gone out of control resulting in an injury to his brother's leg.

Since he had never dreamed precognitively before, Roland asked, should he take this dream seriously enough to give some warning to his brother?

This is a type of question often faced by psychics who sometimes intuitively pick up information about people whether or not they have been requested to do so. Psychic Ray Stanford, for example, tells the story of once having been visited by a group of high school boys who were interested, as he was, in unidentified flying objects.

Looking at one of the boys, Stanford noticed the absence of an aura (the energy field which surrounds the body perceivable to many with so-called "second sight"). Stanford drew the boy's friends aside and told them that their friend would meet with death within a few days. The boys were unbelieving since to their knowledge all was well with their friend. However, two days later he was dead, killed by his father in a tragic accident.

The rule of thumb which applies to warning others of a precognition seems to be that: one, if you have a strong feeling of its being accurate and two, if you feel that the person warned might possibly make use of the information to alter the situation, go ahead and risk telling it. Any forewarning should certainly be preceeded with an explanation of how the information was received and that it could possibly be distorted by your own perceptions.

Which brings us to the question of distortion. Relatively few people I have met either in workshops or among my friends have dreams with any frequency which are clearly and on a one-to-one-basis precognitive; yet, as I sometimes do, it is possible to wake with the feeling that some part of a dream or some part of the message of a dream might be precognitive even though it is mingled with other dream elements.

One woman I met in a workshop, for example, quite frequently would dream about a fire or an airplane crash or some other emotion-laden event, knowing that somewhere at sometime the event would occur but not knowing enough to take any reasonable steps for its prevention.

Another person told me that he had dreamed more than once of the deaths of close friends or relatives, feeling the truth of the dream so thoroughly that he was directed to inform the person of it, only to be proven false time and again.

What are the reasons for such happenings? First, if it is true that we create our own reality in waking consciousness (and remember we are operating on that theory), then it *must* be true that we create our own reality at the dream level and even the most accurate of precognitive dreams comes to our awareness for some strictly personal reason as well as any reason that may be helpful to someone else.

Why, I asked the woman in the workshop, and well she might ask herself, did she dream of fires and airplane crashes; and why would someone dream about the death of a friend or relative? There are two possible explanations I can think of. One is that these events are particular symbols to the dreamer. If it is true that we create our own reality even in the waking world, and that those events which we face in our daily life, whether they be love or strife, are reflections of our inner thoughts and energies, then how true it must be that the events upon which we choose to focus in our dreams must also be a reflection, a product of the inner workings of our consciousness. The person who dreams of fires or accidents or death may be choosing these events as symbols of internal fears, anxieties or wishes which have to do only peripherally with the person or thing dreamed about.

The second explanation, of course, is that the dreamer is accurately perceiving the thoughts or emotions of another; that because of the dreamer's sensitivity, the unspoken, even unconscious feelings of another person might be received.

I am reminded of a lucid dream I once had in which my friend Noreen appeared, or rather I appeared in her house. Since I was aware that I was dreaming, I said to her, "Are you really you, or are you just my creation of you?"

"A little of both," she laughed, and proceeded to change form in front of me.

And here, I think is one of the keys to the idea of creating our own reality whether in dreams or while awake. It is not an individual effort. We create our piece of reality while all of those around us are equally creating or perceiving, and that which we create or perceive is that which is meaningful to us even though it may at the same time be meaningful to another person.

This is also the answer to the question of whether or not to tell someone else about a precognitive dream. We *can* learn to determine whether the dream is a "true" dream, or a dream which might happen in daily life; we can learn by trial and error, by being aware of our dreams, and by measuring the emotional connotation or impact the dream has on us. But whether or not the dream is one which comes true in the everyday world, it *always* has a meaning and importance to you, for you are the dreamer and you select your dreams.

The importance of this statement was brought home to me once when I awoke from a particularly vivid lucid dream which I intended to ask the friend who appeared in it if he remembered. I awoke with a single, previously unheard of, phrase repeating itself in my mind like a South American proverb: "May the life of the sweeper change the width of the broom."

And I think that is a particularly important thing for us all to remember—that no matter how phenomenal the dream, how dramatic, that every dream, every experience is particularly ours to learn from, to grow from, to change that which needs to be changed and enjoy what is ours to enjoy, because it is our own life that does "change the width of the broom."

There is a fine dream story which is particularly applicable to this question of distortion and the possibility of distorting what may be a valid prediction by something which is strictly personal.

The first year I lived in Virginia Beach, in 1973, I was teaching in a local high school. Between dreams I heard from my students, and other teachers and dreams I heard from my friends in other parts of the city, I realized that around Christmas-time that year I was hearing a large number of dreams about tidal waves. In fact I had one myself. The typical dream found the dreamer standing on the beach while an absolutely gigantic wave crested in the immediate vicinity, sometimes washing everything away, sometimes just flooding everything. I must have heard no fewer than fifteen tidal wave dreams in a two-or-three-week period, and I wasn't looking for them.

Those who are interested in things psychic may be aware that Edgar Cayce was told by his own source, or the guidance of his readings, that he should move to Virginia Beach because not only was the proximity of the Atlantic Ocean conducive to the giving of psychic readings, but that Virginia Beach would be a particularly safe area in times of the coming "earth changes." Not only Cayce, but innumerable other psychics both well known and not so well known have predicted that before the year 2,000 the coming Aquarian Age might be heralded by a series of physical earth upheavals which could destory major areas in all parts of the globe. Thus I was not particularly surprised when a few days after I heard the tidal wave dreams, the rumor began to spread that Virginia Beach was in for a tidal wave that Christmas. Some people made a point to leave town for the holidays. But alas, nothing happened.

After that I noticed that every year around that same time I heard the usual spate of tidal wave dreams.

In December of 1977 Poseidia Institute sponsored a three-session Psychic Seminar to which all of the practicing psychics in the Tidewater Area were invited, to discuss the trials and tribulations as well as the joys of being a psychic. Because Virginia Beach is well populated with people who are interested in developing their intuitive abilities, even without those who refused the invitation we had an average crowd of around twenty people at the seminar. And at the last of these sessions the psychics discussed the question of distortion: What to do if you feel the information is accurate but it turns out not to be; how to handle the problem of some people's blind faith in a psychic's ability; how to overcome fears of giving misinformation (a fear which every honest psychic faces). The group was very much in favor of helping the individuals in it work through these problems.

The next day, December 21st, brought a surprise. One of the psychics who had attended the seminar had had a vision (similar to a dream). He had received the information that there was going to be a tidal wave and had learned exactly what date and time it would occur. Alarmed and concerned he ran off dozens of posters announcing the coming event and posted them throughout the town.

The date predicted came, and the time, but the tidal wave did not. The next day a very embarrassed psychic replaced posters all over town with a note of apology.

What was the meaning of this failure? How many prophets have led their followers to the mountaintop only to find that the prophesied doomsday does not arrive? Does it mean that there is no such thing as accurate prophecy, or that these people are charlatans? We have proven that some precognitions can in fact be very accurate. I think rather that, like the many dreamers who dreamed the tidal wave dream each Christmas in Virginia Beach, there was no real attempt to deceive on the part of the psychic under discussion, but more probably a misinterpretation, a distortion if you will, of the information perceived.

The dreamers may well have been perceiving a "real" event which did not have sufficient energy to manifest itself in this physical reality system; and moreover, at a personal level the dream may be highly significant. At what more appropriate time than the Christmas season and the coming of a New Year, could the dreamer's thoughts turn to the coming of the huge wave, which to many bespeaks spirit and spiritual cleansing, which would wash away or clean up the debris of a past year?

I am convinced that with practice, and with some daring, it is possible to determine which of our dreams are talking about something which may happen to us or someone else in waking reality, and what should be interpreted at a more personally symbolic level. The psychics call this developing clarity.

And, while we are talking about clarity, I think we should touch upon another type of dream which seems to me to be far more common than current dream literature would have us believe, and that is the dream about someone who is dead—not just a dream in which that person appears, but a dream in which the person comes to give a particular message.

Of course, according to more conventional theories, there is no such things as communicating with the "dead," and anyone who does so, even in dreams, is certainly suspect. Yet according to Jane Roberts and Seth, "You are as dead now as you'll ever be," and, along the lines of the theory which we are discussing, this makes a certain amount of sense.

If you are not your body, but your body is a vehicle formed by your consciousness as a symbol, as a certain type of tool for learning certain experiences, then what we call the death of the body by no means indicates the death of consciousness but merely a refocusing of it; and there is no reason to believe that our consciousness would not use a similar "body" as a symbol in other areas of consciousness. Another way of saying this is that a "ghost" is just as real as we are, only existing in an area of time and space which we do not ordinarily perceive with our physical senses.

How many stories have you heard of friends or relatives who have seen a dead person, generally someone close to them, in a dream? I have heard literally dozens. And does it seem more logical to tell these people (as many tell me they have been told by comforting friends or well-meaning psychiatrists) that this is just a symptom of their grief, that it isn't real, or (at worst) that they'd better snap out of it or they will find themselves in an institution? Or does it seem logical to think that if a large number of otherwise apparently sane, rational, "normal" humans share the same logical experience it might be worth investigating the premise that created the doubt about its being logical in the first place?

Susan was a student in one of the high school classes I taught. At sixteen she was exceptionally pretty, a cheerleader, a member of the high school student government and a straight A student. When the class began to talk about dreams, it was Susan who asked rather timidly if anyone else had ever dreamed about someone who died. Though no one in the group had had that experience they listened with interest as Susan told her story.

Susan was very close to her grandmother, who died when she was eleven years old. The grandmother lived on a farm where Susan and her brothers and sisters often visited, sometimes spending part of their summer holidays there.

After her grandmother's death, Susan said, she would often dream that she was in the barn at her grandmother's farm where her grandmother would come in and they would talk as they had when her grandmother was alive. As time went on Susan would frequently take the problems she was facing in her waking life to the grandmother she met in her dreams for discussion and sensible solution. The only time she mentioned this to her family, they had been amused and then worried; so, she told the class, she stopped talking about it.

Louise, a competent social worker who had been working in Juvenile Services for some years with a record of capable and effective problem solving for pre-delinquent teenagers, told me that she was still in college and living at home when her father died. The family had been an exceptionally close-knit one and her mother many months later was still very grieved, finding it difficult to find meaning in her life now that her husband was gone.

Louise said that despite the fact that her father was dead she frequently saw him or heard him around the house and felt his presence nearby. She explained to me that she hadn't mentioned this to anyone because "they would have worried about me."

Finally another man became interested in the mother and she was also interested in him, but did not want to be disloyal to the memory of her dead husband. Louise said that her father came to her in a dream "as real as we are sitting here," and said, emphatically, "Tell you mother to remarry and enjoy her life!" After some persuasion, Louise said, her mother did just that.

Tom was so close to his adopted young son Tommy that when he and his wife divorced, despite the fact that he gave up custody of their two other children, he wanted to keep Tommy with him. It was not easy for these two since the father had to work and the child had been ill since his birth with a glandular disorder which sometimes sent him into convulsions. Yet they were very close and helped each other through the tough times.

When Tommy was seven, Tom remarried. Shortly after the marriage, Tommy had a convulsion and went into a coma in his sleep. No one heard him, and by the time the child was found the next morning the doctors were unable to revive him. The father was almost insensible with grief, and relatives feared he might try to take his own life.

Weeks passed and every morning at exactly the same time, the father would wake from a nightmare of reliving the episode of how the boy had been found in a coma. He was haggard and hated to go to sleep at night. Finally, he recounted, waking one morning he saw Tommy sitting in a chair at the foot of the bed. The boy said nothing, but smiled sweetly and at last the father knew he was well and safe. Though the grief remained at no longer having his son with him, Tom was able to realize that Tommy was happy and wanted him to be happy, too.

An interesting sidelight of this story is that Tom, whose relatives really thought he had cracked under the stress, said that during his first marriage he and his family had lived in a "haunted" house and that they often heard footsteps and sometimes the sound of laughter or crying.

When Tommy was a small child in this house, Tom said, his bedroom door had been left open and the light on so they could listen for sounds of difficulty he might have. This particular night both Tom and his wife had been sleeping soundly when, Tom said, someone shook him hard enough to shake the bed. Both Tom and his wife were awakened by this shaking, yet when Tom turned on the light no one was there. Tom's first thought was Tommy and though he heard no sound, he rushed down the hall to the child's room and again found him in a coma from which he was saved due to their discovering it, and speedy work in the hospital emergency room.

Now, the question is should we consider these people crazy or deluded or unstable, perhaps suffering from a type of hallucination? Or might we consider that the dreams and visions they perceived were perfectly ordinary and accurate?

A philosophy which insists that dead is dead and that dreams are meaningless or imaginary or at best strictly symbolic, cannot, of course, incorporate these experiences with discarnate individuals as anything but hallucinatory.

Yet if it should be true that what we perceive as time and space are simply illusory barriers, then death in the physical sense has very little meaning except for loss of the atoms and molecules which we call our physical bodies, and consciousness carries its energies into other dimensions no less "real" than our own; no more disembodied than our own; and certainly perceivable to those who have a close emotional tie.

I will not go into here the reasons for not encouraging a pursuit of emotional ties across the boundaries of physical "death," other than to say that each experience in any reality seems to have its own reason and logic. But the reason might be summed up in the dream report of another individual, a reporter who attended one of my dream workshops. She said that after her father's death she had tried in a variety of ways to communicate with him, feeling guilty about the animosity which had existed between them during his lifetime. Finally her father appeared to her in a dream. "I have no doubt that it was really him," she said. "He was far too real for that."

Her father had asked her sternly, just as he would have had he been alive, to leave him alone because he had other experiences to get on to; and she, by her emotional ties to him, was holding him back.

Chapter Five

Several Types Of Dreams

If you are like I am, the possibility that dreams may be ordinary perceptions of an unordinary reality, in addition to opening up many new doors, may also make the problem of understanding dreams even more difficult in some ways than it was before.

To restate the theory: we create our own reality, each of us, for the purpose of learning and growing; and we create the reality with our thoughts and emotions and beliefs. A group of people together create a group reality; and everything we perceive to be real, whether we are "awake" or "asleep" is part of that reality creation and a symbol of our inner thoughts and feelings. The essential nature of things is oneness; and, in fact, separation into individuals, into time, and into space is an illusion that we have created.

To make this theory more practical and to help myself to understand its application to dreams, I devised, along with several people who participated in dream workshops, some categories into which dreams seem to fall. These are only tentative categories and there may be others, or you may want to call them by other names; but for the sake of this particular work we will explore the following dream categories: (1) self-guidance dreams which I sometimes call progress reports; (2) self-amusement or creativity dreams; (3) problem solving dreams or working things out with another person; (4) dreams for another person; (5) spiritual or visionary dreams; (6) precognitive dreams; and (7) lucid dreaming.

A closer look at these dream categories will reveal that, with the exception of lucid dreams and precognitive dreams which may appear in any of the categories, the definitions move from the strictly personal dream wherein the dreamer is working out a personal problem, to dreams wherein the dreamer is working out something with another person or persons, to the spiritual or visionary dream in which the dreamer encounters what might be called his spiritual essence, God, or other uplifting parts of himself.

It is an ancient concept of Zen Buddhism and other older religions that what is ordinarily perceived as reality in the waking state is illusion; that separateness is an illusion and that, in fact, there is only oneness.

Today from their trance state readings, psychics tell us that the "earth plane" or physical reality is a reality system where dichotomies are perceived instead of unity—good and evil, black and white, man and woman. For every thing there is an opposite, even to the laws of classic physics which state, "For every action there is an equal and opposite reaction."

Psychic Ellen Andrews-Negus says of this state of perception that humanity has separated consciousness into the observer and the observed.

Yet it is also said by today's psychics that the true nature of things is oneness, that all of time and space exist in the present moment and that we are but individualized particles of the same consciousness which we call God. Thus it stands to reason that dreams would cover the spectrum from individualized or personality consciousness to cosmic consciousness, and also that some dreams would come clothed in the symbols of our present moment while others would take on "unfamiliar" or broader symbols.

As I noted earlier, dreams often seem to mix the variety of perceptions, and it is not altogether an easy matter to find dreams which fit strictly into one or another of the categories outlined by workshop participants and myself; yet I will try to give some relatively clear examples of each category. For even many people who have studied dreams for a long time do not acknowledge this expanded pattern of dreaming. And I believe that as long as we are forced to believe that every dream has a one-to-one correlation with emotional events of the present day and can be interpreted only in that light, we are missing half the fun of dreaming—not to mention half the possible value of such activity. I also believe it is possible to determine whether a dream is of one type or another and deal with it accordingly (i.e., it is not necessary to interpret a dream you have had for someone else as symbolic to yourself; but it *is* a good idea to be able to tell the the difference so you don't ignore an important personal message).

Just as for the layman it may be true that one apple is as good as another as an apple is an apple, to the scientist researching new strains of apples it is important to know a Red Delicious from a

Winesap; so, I think, is it true that the serious researcher into dreams needs to be able to distinguish one type of dream or state of consciousness from another.

Self-guidance dreams which I often call progress reports, are the most ordinary types of dream for many people. They can cover the area from the most mundane of subject levels to the most profound. Yet basically they comment on the day-to-day, present-day life of the dreamer.

A few years ago I dreamed the following:

> I was at my mother's house and had gone out the front door for something. At the door I met a young boy. He was carrying a bag of groceries. I let him in the door.
>
> In the next scene I was in a car, going somewhere, riding in the back seat with my mother. Though I wanted to continue on the journey, my mother insisted that I go back to the store and buy some raisins.

At first I didn't understand the implications of the dream and tried to assign it a variety of meanings, but later that week I again dreamed I was at the store buying raisins and the meaning became clear.

Though my mother and the childhood home in which I grew up until I went away to college have a variety of dream meanings for me, one of the most important is as a symbol of childhood authority. At the time of the dream I had been feeling run down and overworked from a heavy teaching load. Again in the automobile, which for me often represents the vehicle of my body, I was taking a back seat, riding with my mother who insisted that, even though I was enjoying my journey, I should go buy some raisins. I finally understood that raisins are rich in iron and that was exactly what I needed to cure my run-down condition. In waking life, I took time to go to the store and buy some raisins as well as some Vitamin B capsules and soon was feeling fine again. Just as in my childhood, my dream mother represented "Mother knows best."

Dreams can frequently give information on how to deal with health problems even before they become evident in waking life, and a later chapter will deal with some people's ability to heal others from the sleep state. One woman I know regularly dreams about the foods she needs to maintain a proper dietary balance. If oranges or Vitamin C are necessary, she dreams about oranges. If it's more green, leafy vegetables, she dreams lettuce or spinach.

This, like other dream events, is a programmable ability. However, it is necessary to make sure what the dream is talking about.

Early in my association with Poseidia Institute I found myself regularly dreaming about chocolate pie. I would find myself in a diner or restaurant with other people I knew, eating chocolate pie—until I began to wonder if it could possibly be that chocolate pie was missing from my diet. Finally, after discussing my dreams with several other people, I realized that I had chosen to symbolize the PI of Poseidia Institute (which had been referred to in readings by the Institute's founder, psychic Mikey McCorkle, as *pi*, or the ratio of the circumference of a circle to its diameter) as "pie"; and I determined that chocolate for me symbolized energy. So, in fact, I was discussing Poseidia Institute in the shorthand of my dreams.

Self-guidance dreams directing or commenting on the direction of one's life can be a great help if the dreamer is willing to explore them in an objective way.

When I spoke earlier about gestalting dreams and/or working with a dream group, this was what I meant. I have often found in the past that dreams with a message that was clear as a bell were misunderstood or overlooked by me simply because in dream life I did not want to get the message any more than I did in waking life.

One such dream occurred in 1972 when I was planning on moving into an intentional community with a group of friends. We had been planning the community for several years, and my waking self felt I had nothing to worry about even though I knew the attrition rate of communities was high. All of us had been friends for two years or more. We had investigated other communities and tried to build safeguards into ours, and we had proceeded with what we felt to be due maturity and caution.

Yet in May before I was to make the final move to the community in June, I had the following dream:

> The house is built and I look out in back. There is a bulldozer there flattening the land, moving it to the back of the property.
> I go out and Jeanne and some others have begun to plant a garden. The dirt is raw. There are four stakes and on top of each stake is a dead fish.

My interpretation of the dream at the time, despite its stark clarity was in terms of growing things and having the community prosper. I wrote, "I don't understand the fish, but the Indians used them as fertilizer."

In retrospect, after the community experience had indeed had a bulldozing effect on my life and left me quite raw, I re-examined the elements of the dream—the four stakes in the garden, four as a foundation number and the four-square foundation being laid. Yet the fish fertilizer, which I had not understood, was on top of the stakes where it could only rot in the sun instead of under the earth where it would have fertilized the garden.

Gardens appear often in my dreams both because I love gardening myself and because they symbolize the fruits of my labors. Had I been a little more aware of what my honest dream self was telling me, or had I had the benefit of a more objective dream group, I might have saved myself a little wear and tear. Of course, it can always be argued that experience is the best teacher; but it is my contention that, once having experienced the results of an action in the dream state, we may not necessarily have to attempt the same action in the waking state.

Nightmares are the voice of the dream self shouting to be heard—the progress report dream carried to its ultimate conclusion. I have spoken with many, many people who have experienced recurring dreams of a traumatic sort or what they called nightmares from which they awake screaming or trembling.

Once the self-guiding principle of dreams has reached the nightmare stage, it *must* signify a deep underlying conflict, and may need the assistance of an objective other person such as a psychiatrist or counselor to help straighten it out.

Many, many children and young people experience nightmares, and I am amazed to discover that these so often go unnoticed or are dealt with as "just dreams."

One of the correlatives of the psychic theory that all of time and space is happening in the present moment is that the entity which is "born" into the present physical reality as a child comes equipped with a consciousness that is much closer to an awareness of the other elements of time and space than the average adult, and there is much evidence to support this idea if we are willing to open our eyes to it.

The number of children who, independent of one another, have "invisible playmates," for example, is significant even though in most cases parents accept these playmates as amusing or annoying. Yet almost every psychic I have ever met admits to such playmates when they were children, whether or not they told their parents about them. These playmates were "real" people who could be seen and heard by the psychic in question even though they were invisible to others.

I have a friend in the theatre, a director, who once conducted a workshop for young children at a well-known New England drama camp. To introduce the children in the workshop to the stage, and to make them comfortable with speaking from the stage, he asked his young audience how many of them had invisible playmates. Well over half of the hands went up. Somewhat surprised, he asked some of the children to describe their invisible friends as the first exercise in being on stage. Then curious, he asked the other children, most of whom were thoroughly unfamiliar with one another, if they could see each other's invisible friends. Some said they could and the descriptions which followed indicated that, even though to my director friend the characters were invisible, to many in the room they were not.

If it is true that children are accustomed to operating with a broader perceptual framework than the average adult, then we must assume that the experience of adult lack of awareness can at times be upsetting if not downright terrifying.

In a series of beautifully written books, the British authoress and psychic, Joan Grant, gives an insight into what might be done to help children through some of the traumas of transferring from one reality system to the other, discussing in such books as *The Eyes of Horus*, a fiction-like tale of ancient Egypt, the use of animal pets to reduce childhood fears and the fact of how unthinking adults can sometimes instill fears in a child which do not surface until the more experimental world of dreams, i.e., "If you walk on that wall you can fall and break your back;" "If you eat that it will poison you;" "The bogey man will get you if you keep it up."

If it is true that thought creates things, then children are, if anything, more likely than adults to create fearsome thought forms from a world which is strange and different to them.

One way to deal with nightmares is discussed by Dr. Patricia Garfield in her book *Creative Dreaming* where she tells of a psychiatrist's work with a young boy who is chased in his dreams by a monster. The doctor gained the child's trust by becoming his guide and accomplice in chasing the animal away, first in imaginary sessions in the office and then in the dream itself.

Another way of coping with nightmare fears is a way chosen by a group of people with whom I am familiar. Thea, age five, ordinarily a happy and well-adjusted child, was regularly waking up screaming from the nightmare that there was someone in her room. Leaving the light on and the door open seemed to do no good at all.

One evening about a week after the dreams began, a study group of which her mother was a member met in their home. The mother explained what had been happening. During the meditation that evening, one of the group members with decided psychic talents went into trance. When she came out of the trance she explained she had "seen" someone in the room in which the child slept, and described her. The mother in surprise recounted that a close friend of hers in another city had committed suicide quite recently and that she, in fact, had dreamed about the woman a few days earlier but had attributed the dream to her knowledge of her friend's death.

The group, in a prayer session after the meeting, prayed that the woman be released from the trauma of her suicide and that friends on the "other side" (a term sometimes used to describe the location of consciousness of those who have left the earth) would come and help her.

Thea's nightmares ceased.

It seems undeniably true that, as a society, we pay pitifully little attention to our dreams and the dreams of our children. In certain "primitive" tribes such as the Senoi of Malaysia (as reported by Kilton Stewart in the 1930's) dreams are an integral part of the workings of the society and each morning at breakfast chidren are encouraged to share their dreams with the rest of the family and utilize their dreams for personal growth. One wonders how much more well adjusted children might be in our civilized society if such attention were given to dreams and other extraordinary experiences.

Another nightmare time, in more than one sense of the word, seems to be puberty and early adolescence. I have spoken with many teenagers and even more adults who have recounted that this time of life brought nightmares of being chased, attacked, laughed at or mobbed. The usual comment from adults is that they "eventually outgrew" such dreams; and that may well be the case.

We often call teenagers sensitive, and there is no denying that many are; but what is done to help people through this trying time? If it is true that the nightmare is the self-guidance dream carried to its ultimate extent, what can be done to help people past the nightmare stage?

Even the nightmare can be interpreted as the message the inner self is attempting to give to the outer self; and if the adolescent dreams, as one burly, football-playing youngster did in one of my writing classes (who, incidentally, said he never dreamed, but after others in the class began to talk of their experiences "remembered" that he'd had this recurrently) that a nuclear bomb had exploded and he felt the flame as he watched his house and his family be blown away, can't we help him see it as more than stupid or crazy, but an important message?

This particular boy was nearing graduation and, as it was prior to the revocation of the draft, would soon be faced with the decision of whether to go to college, which he really did not want to do, or enlist before he was drafted, a possibility which he saw as terrifying because he had grown up with tales of war and nuclear holocaust.

Even though the other students had little to offer him by way of resolving his dilemma, he learned through class discussion that not only did they not consider his dream as stupid as he thought, but many of his classmates silently shared his fears.

The nightmare, he reported later, did not return in that form. Unfortunately because this was a public school English class, there was no opportunity to probe into the deeper elements of chaos which I suspect were lurking there in the dream as a result of an extremely explosive family situation; but had there been the opportunity one might have helped this "normal, well-adjusted" high schooler toward an understanding of his problems and the resolution of them.

Dreams for self-amusement and creativity, unlike the frequently serious self-guidance dream, have a playful quality.

Just as in some workshops where I ask people to list their three best qualities and leave them stammering and blushing when many could go on for hours about their worst qualities; so, I think, does the serious dreamer often get involved in the belief that dreaming is a serious business, designed to uncover the deepest and therefore the darkest recesses of our hidden selves. There is, I'm afraid, a great deal of the old Protestant work ethic left in the best of us; and to suggest that many dreams are for the sheer purpose of enjoyment and entertainment is to utter something of a blasphemy.

Yet that seems to be the case. And if it is true that we create our own reality, surely it is true that the underlying basis of creativity is joyfulness and harmony. Though it is certainly possible to look at a dream and explain in the best royal tradition, "We are not amused," how can one explain such dreams as the following:

I was walking toward the barn when a large black cat passed me. I greeted it. It greeted me. I got to the barn and someone was letting the animals out. I began to help. There was a pair of lions, horses, other farm animals, then bison and even elephants, all lumbering and racing out of the barn in joyous abandon at their freedom.

Now granted, the serious dream interpreter, and I mean the one who approaches the subject with a long face, could interpret the dream as my release of my animal passions, which I'm sure it was; but how does one deal with the sheer abandon of the animals and the joyous feeling of the dream other than by categorizing it—dreams for joy and amusement?

A friend of mine once told me that she fell asleep staring out the window at the panoply of stars, wondering what it would be like to fly among them when suddenly she found herself aloft and heading toward the nearest star. Made a little nervous by the flight, she looked back toward earth but then summoned her courage and headed out toward the Milky Way.

Many people discuss the experience of flying in their dreams and, though some psychiatric literature would have us believe that the flying dream is integrally connected with messages of sexuality, the most common expression I have encounted about dreams of flying, including flying in lucid dreams, is that it is great fun and the dreamer looks forward to doing it with delight.

Once when I was appearing on a television talk show to talk about dreams, my host and hostess began even before the program went on the air to discuss dreams they had had. Naturally, the first question that came up was about dreams of flying. I asked the T.V. hostess if she was aware she was dreaming when she was dreaming. "Of course," she replied, as if this were the most commonplace thing in the world.

And did she often have dreams of flying? Well, she said, she used to until a friend told her she shouldn't have. More's the pity for this woman who so obviously loved to dream for her own amusement, and for the friend who apparently believed there was something wrong in doing so.

Do these dreams have deep meanings, or discuss fears and anxieties? To the extent that they show us joyful and creative alternatives to fear and anxiety, they do.

Dreams used for artistic creation also fit into this category, and are interesting enough to merit a whole chapter in this book, but I will give a few examples here.

Author Andre Sonnet recounts in his book *The Twilight Zone of Dreams* the story of how Danish nuclear physicist and Nobel Laureate Niels Bohr discovered the interatomic arrangement of molecules, the Bohr atomic model, which made him famous.

Bohr, who often told the tale himself, had been working day and night on the problem of molecule arrangement when one night he dreamed the solution to the problem. "As he put it," Sonnet recounts, "it was as though he suddenly witnessed the superhuman showmanship of elementary particles with electrons racing around their nuclei with unimaginable speed, following their eternal path."

Another scientist, a chemistry professor and personal friend of mine who also dreams creatively, solved a less earth-shattering but equally pleasing enigma a few years ago when he and his office partner planned to put on one of their regular productions of a chemistry-based alchemy show.

Days before the performance one of the chemical compounds used to produce the magical effects in the alchemy show simply wasn't working, and no matter what the two professors did to induce it to work, nothing happened.

More and more worried as the date of the show drew near, my friend had a simple, straightforward dream one night that told him the compound had been incorrectly mixed at the professional laboratory where the chemicals had been purchased.

By this time he was ready to believe anything. He telephoned the laboratory, asked a few questions about the preparation of the compound, and sure enough, his dream was correct. The compound was reformulated and worked perfectly.

It is difficult for me to fit such matter-of-fact problem solutions or creative acts into a theory of dreams such as the ancient one which says either that dreams are the meaningless wanderings of the chemical elements of the brain and body left to rest, or the more modern theory that dreams are the ramblings of the mind over events in our daily lives. My friend had no awareness of how the chemical had been compounded in the laboratory, yet he used the intuitive flexibility of the dream state to solve his problem.

Only the more complex theory that dreams present us with an extended awareness of the true nature of reality seems to work. Both of the above dreams did deal with certain problems current in the daily lives of the dreamer. However, the dreams themselves touched upon solutions which had not been apparent in waking life, and in fact contained elements of "reality" which are not considered available to us in waking life. In one case it was a vision of sub-microscopic particles, and in the other it was "unavailable" information on the mixture of a compound. Lucky guesses? If this is true, the number of individuals who are inherently capable of such luck or who can train themselves to it seems phenomenal.

Working out problems with other people, or what one of my friends calls *instant replay dreams,* seems to be one of the most popular categories of dreams as we move along the spectrum from observer to observed, or diversity to unity.

Many people have told me that their dream life is exactly like their waking life, in that there are absolutely no extraordinary elements in them whatsoever—no flying, no fluid changing of one dream element into another, no rapid change of location or bizarre characters.

Dreams, they say, are precisely like waking life except that the same event which happened during the day may have a different outcome at night, or something planned for tomorrow may be previewed in the dream.

Though to me this seems extraordinarily dull, and I wonder if these people don't simply forget their flights of fancy. There is no denying that this type of dreaming suits almost perfectly the Cayce adage that nothing happens in waking life without having first been dreamed.

I am sure that many times in dreams we are simply exploring the probable outcome of a variety of experiences.

What classic dream scholars call *wish fulfillment dreams*, I think often fit into this category (if not into the category of self-amusement) since frequently behavior accepted as normal and socially acceptable in the dream world is considered abnormal or very socially unacceptable in the world of waking reality.

Thus in dreams it is possible to explore the possibility of arguing with the boss, of gaining ascendancy over a rival, of making love with someone, or in some cases of even doing away with an unwanted foe, with none of the usual recriminations. The person who is very exhausted or weary of a particular action may find a dream life filled with repetitions of that same action ad infinitum and ad nauseum.

Yet, in my opinion it is possible to go much farther than this with the working out or instant replay dream.

If it is true, as the psychics tell us, that time and space are illusion; and if, as psychics prove time and again, we are very much in contact with each other's minds every moment whether or not we are consciously aware of it, then the working-out dream becomes a vehicle for communication. I believe it is impossible for one of us to deal with another of us on any level without a correspondent recognition in the other person.

In dreams, I often find myself among the same people with whom I spend my days. We talk about a mutual problem or take action on something that has involved us in waking life.

Whereas in many cases in waking life it is inappropriate to discuss a particular situation or feeling, this can be done with ease in the dream world. It is as possible to program dream solutions to difficulties in inter-personal relationships as it is possible to program creative solutions to artistic problems. If, for example, in waking life there has been an argument or a misunderstanding but one with which you truly wish to deal, then by the act of programming a solution, by repeating before sleep the desire to work the problem out, you may be surprised at the result. I have on occasion found myself apologizing in dreams for something which in waking life I would neither admit was my fault nor be willing to set aside my pride to apologize for.

Yet the result of such activity you may find to be truly remarkable especially if it is a situation which is difficult to handle in any other way.

A perfect example of such a case came while I was teaching in public school. In one particular class I had a student, a boy who was very bright but always sullen and rude. I'll call him Keith. He was enough of a leader that dealing with the class was always a delicate situation. If I came down too hard on this boy about doing something distracting, or not working, other boys in the class would rally around him and come to his defense. If I did nothing about his behavior, others would take it as a signal that they could copy him. I was constantly puzzled by what to do and thought about the situation a great deal until one night I recorded the following dream.

I was walking down the street near my mother's house. It was dark. When I got just about to Hahn's place, a gang of boys came out of the bushes. I tried to pretend I didn't notice them and just kept walking, but they were advancing toward me. I was frightened. Their leader was Keith.

Finally I confronted Keith and gave him a real tongue lashing. I was shaking my finger at him and shouting, saying you just can't do that anymore. I began to beat on his chest in frustration (in dream life I was quite a lot smaller than he is just like in waking life) and cry.

When I did that he became very apologetic and very protective. He called off his gang.

I could have accepted this as just a replay of my frustration with this particular student except that from the time of that dream his behavior toward me changed radically. None of the other factors had changed. He was still in the same class with the same other students, the same subject matter and, obviously, the same teacher. Yet he began to accept me as another human being and not the teacher role to which he had been reacting. Though he was never a model student, in waking life he also "called off his gang" and sometimes even exercised his good mind to the surprise of the other students.

I am not saying that the dream was an isolated event. Probably several weeks of trying to show my concern and frustration finally made their impact as possibly did his underlying desire to be loved and accepted. Yet there is no doubt in my mind that the dream encounter was as real and productive, if not more so, then the encounters in the waking world.

Dreams for another person are a sometimes puzzling dream category in relationship to dreams which work things out with another. This is a rather tricky category, but one which I feel should be discussed. Precognitive dreams for another person are only one possibility in this category, being a clear warning about some event which will probably take place.

As I said earlier every dreamer peoples his dream world with certain characters for certain reasons, and certainly every dream can be interpreted as having a message for the dreamer. Yet some dreams, despite this rather psychoanalytic theory, undoubtedly contain messages of meaning for another person, sometimes even simple messages as the two dream examples given here; and if the person dreamed about is receptive to the message, there is probably no harm in giving it.

One example dream occurred in my life about two years ago:

> I was standing in a storeroom in front of a wall of shelves. On the top shelf were several hams. They were rocking back and forth. Someone remarked, "This is getting out of hand. The hams are dancing." A woman I know only slightly, Mrs. A., was standing beside me.
> I held out my hands. Eileen (a friend of mine) handed me a blue fish.

The message was fairly clear to me that I had been eating a lot of pork, which never agrees with my digestive system, and things were beginning to get out of hand. Eileen, being a psychic who frequently does medical readings of a nature comparable to those of Edgar Cayce, represented the intuitive side of myself telling me that a meal of bluefish would be much healthier.

I was left, then, with the question of Mrs. A. What was she doing in my dream? She had no particular symbolic significance for me, and played no active part in the dream but was instead a listener.

Mrs. A came up in conversation with a mutual friend a few days later and I mentioned the dream. The friend said, "That's interesting. Mrs. A. was telling me just yesterday about the magnificent ham she fixed over the weekend." I could only conclude that the dream message for Mrs. A., as well as myself, might be that bluefish would be better and suggested to our mutual friend that she could mention the dream message if it seemed appropriate.

Another example of dreaming for another person came from a friend of mine who called me one evening after she had awakened from a nap. "I just had a dream," she said, "and it doesn't seem to have any particular meaning for me. Maybe it does for you." The dream she recounted was this:

She had been walking along the beach and had come upon me and a group of other Poseidia Institute members. I was directing these people to decorate a large wave-like structure built of sand with seafoam of various beautiful shades of pink and green. There was going to be a festival. The structure was very large and very beautiful.

But as my friend passed under the structure and came to the other side of it, a sibyl-type of person said to her that this had been done before some time ago, and that the structure had collapsed, killing several people. If I continued, the sibyl said, it could happen again. The sand structure needed to be built slowly and watered carefully every day until it was rock hard and firm or again the collapse would come. This time people would not be killed, but the structure could be ruined and people would be hurt.

Whether or not the dream contained any signifcant information for my friend (and I suspect it did) there was definitely a message there for me. I had in fact been driving the Institute's staff of paid and volunteer personnel quite hard to build the structure of the organization and not really paying enough attention to details of personal health and comfort. This and other messages I had been receiving from myself and others caused me to stand back from what I had been doing and move more slowly—if not seeming to accomplish as much, at least building a sound structure.

Spiritual or visionary dreams, called by some writers "high dreams," are, if I am to believe the dreamers with whom I've conversed and corresponded, not at all an unusual category of dreams.

The thing that sets the visionary dream apart is its quality. Generally the dreamer awakes in a state of euphoria, having experienced something that was extremely edifying or enlightening. The content of these dreams varies greatly and depends, as any dream does, upon the dreamer; but the element of having "seen God" or experienced enlightenment is a common denominator. The dreams themselves may or may not have an interpretable symbolic content and may or may not contain a prophetic message.

One man I know dreamed he was pushing a cart down a difficult road when he encountered a shining being, Jesus, who helped him with his heavy load. Another such dream occurred to me when I first began having lucid dreams.

I "awoke" in the dream state and put my hand through the covers to denote that I was dreaming, and left my bed to go to the living room.

When I got there, I found the room was filled with light, brighter than sunlight, coming through the windows and coming through the walls themselves, bouncing off the mirror above the mantle. There was music in the air and the sound of dozens of bells ringing. I was thoroughly elated and found myself bouncing from the floor, floating upwards, and returning to bounce again, chanting, "Bells, bells, bells." I awoke thoroughly ecstatic, feeling as if the world was a wonderful place to be.

Yet another friend of mine loves the dawn and says he was in a semi-sleep state one spring morning when he heard the first sleepy bird begin to chirp, then another. "It was like an orchestra tuning up," he said, "with the violins and one off-beat bass." Then the orchestra began to play and he heard the birds in a gigantic piece of uplifting music. A voice said to him, "You are in the presence."

Later, my friend said, he interpreted what he had heard as meaning, "You are in the present," or the present moment, as he realized fully for the first time that every day is the dawning of a new creation.

The ancients believed that the person was divided into three major components—body, mind or emotions, and spirit—and that in order to deal with the whole peson, one had to deal with all of these elements. Even if it is true that we are at some level all one and that time and space are only constructs we have built for our own learning process, we must admit the vision that we ordinarily perceive in order to deal with them and reach a synthesis.

The first categories named in this chapter (self-guidance dreams, self-amusement or creativity dreams, problem solving or working things out with another, dreams for another, and spiritual or visionary dreams) are, I believe, representative of the various ways the individual chooses ordinarily to perceive himself and his world—the observer and the observed.

The final categories, precognitive dreams and lucid dreams, cross the boundaries of the first five categories into the realms of non-ordinary perception, pointing out the unity we have with one another and the creative force, and the potential capabilities available to humanity.

An example of how *precognitive dreaming* crosses the boundaries of the other categories was given to me by a correspondent from Richmond, Virginia, who said that in the early 1970's, he fell prey to a series of debilitating illnesses that left him in a weakened condition. Doctor after doctor who saw the man could not determine the cause of the illness, but he continued to grow weaker.

Finally, he had a dream. All he recalled was seeing in red letters several feet tall the word ACUPUNCTURE. Being in the field of medicine himself, the man had had conversations with his colleagues about the Oriental medical art of using needles inserted under the skin for cure and control of disease but had scoffed at the idea, as had his friends. However, now, unhelped as he was by traditional Western medicine, he was willing to accept the advice of his dream. He went to a practitioner of acupuncture in Washington, D.C., and soon was feeling as well as he ever had in his life.

The dream, a self-guidance dream, was also precognitive in the sense that it discussed the future.

There are other dreams as well, not necessarily precognitive, which demonstrate non-ordinary perceptions, such as ESP. Mutual dreams are probably the best example of this, dreams in which two or more people share the same dream or elements of the same dream, though not necessarily a dream about the future.

Husbands and wives or members of the same family most frequently seem to report this kind of dream, though mutual dreaming is by no means confined to people with family relationships. And, of course, the fact that we tend to discuss dreams irregularly and infrequently contributes to the possibility that there may be much more mutual dreaming than we have record of. The dream I mentioned earlier between my friend, her husband and myself is an example of mutual dreaming. The number of dreams reported concerning the assassination in 1963 of President John F. Kennedy are also examples with the common factor that they were also precognitive.

Remember that here I am simply trying to list some broad categories of dreams for the purpose of trying to help sort out the mass of available information.

Lucid dreaming, called by some psychic researchers *borderland dreams*, which were discussed in an earlier chapter of this book, is the final dream category.

In my opinion, lucid dreaming is a step in awareness that what we call reality is only a fragment of a greater reality because it begins to create a conscious awareness that indeed we can "be in more than one place at a time" and that space, in some states of consciousness, is no more insurmountable than the nearest thought.

In his book, *Autobiography of a Yogi*, Paramahansa Yogananda describes several of his teachers, including his *guru*, Swami Pranabananda. These men were trained in the ancient Indian tradition of yoga and, though they were living in the 20th century (Yogananda himself died only in 1952), displayed the characteristics ascribed to many saints in the Christian tradition and masters of the physical plane discussed in all religious traditions.

It was possible, according to Yogananda, for these individuals to bi-locate, to be seen in more than one place at a time; to direct their energies toward healing the sick; to foretell the future and perceive events which were happening in other localities many miles away.

There are significant similarities between the meditative state practiced by yogis and others, the trance state practiced by trance psychics, and the dream state. In all three of these states, the functioning of the left hemisphere of the brain, which controls rational thinking and associative logic, is relaxed while the functioning of the right hemisphere of the brain controlling intuition is increased.

When the Yaqui Indian Don Juan told Carlos Castaneda that there was dreaming and then there was *dreaming*, he appears to have been indicating this state, and Castaneda's *Tales of Power* includes one of the best discourses in existence on the subject of how to reach the state of lucid dreams, taking the dreamer step-by-step from just an awareness of being in the dream state to techniques for locating a particular individual in a particular location in this dream state.

The major difference, of course, between the case of bi-location discussed by Yogananda and the lucid dream visit is the ability of the individual to be perceived in what would be called ordinary reality—that is, in cases of bi-location, people who are wide awake report having seen the same individual at widely distant locations exactly the same moment in time (this phenomenon is not nearly so extraordinary as it sounds and many cases are recorded from eminently reliable witnesses in the annals of parapsychology study even though most of the persons who have been observed in such bi-location do not have the conscious control of that ability which yogis purport to have) whereas bi-location in the lucid dream state is usually not witnessed by those who are awake in ordinary reality but takes place while the two people are asleep and is recalled when they awaken.

In his book *Astral Projection*, author and philosopher Oliver Fox recorded several such instances both in the dream state and a trance state he achieved by lying down and relaxing, where he would meet with friends at prearranged times. He also recorded at least one instance where he found himself in another time and place where he was recognized by a group of ecstatic devotees as their "master" returned from the dead.

Such cases sound to us unusual at best and, at worst, the wanderings of deranged minds. Yet there are literally hundreds of cases of such experiences recorded in various books and journals.

The line here, when it comes to the development of such abilities, becomes a very thin one between religious philosophy and various attempts to "know God" and phenomenology or the science of phenomena; and since this is neither a religious text nor a particularly scientific one, I will not got any farther than to state that without exception all religions record cases of individuals who seemed to defy known laws of time and space, that psychics as well as some modern physicists declare that our perception of time and space are illusory; and that dreams, particularly lucid dreams, seem to be a bridge between ordinary and expanded states of consciousness.

Recently there has begun to creep into dream literature the record of some attempts at mutual lucid dreaming. Recent publications of the Bench Press, a small publishing house in Oakland, California, have discussed the use of the martial art form of Tai Chi to induce lucid dreaming in a small group of mutual dreamers; and author James Donahoe discusses the subjects of mutual and lucid dreaming in his excellent book *Dream Reality*, published by the same press.

At Poseidia Institute a group of ten lucid dreamers have been involved in a six-month project of attempting mutual lucid dreaming to investigate how the phenomenon works. All of these researches should provide interesting material for further investigation.

Is it possible to change from one type of dreaming to another? is a question which people frequently ask me. The answer is yes; just as it is possible to start recalling dreams after years of not paying them any heed, it is possible by work, programming and readiness to switch from one type of dreaming to another.

Two rather dramatic cases of switching from one type of dreaming to another came from individuals who were students in my classes at Poseidia Institute.

The first was the individual mentioned in Chapter One who regularly dreamed battlefield scenes until he recognized his own battle with himself and began to deal with it.

After a few weeks of decoding his dreams as they reflected his struggle to come to a better understanding of himself, this individual sat in on a workshop where part of the discussion centered around simplifying the dream message. Participants in the workshop gave various techniques they had used for getting their dreams to give them clearer, more straightforward messages about themselves.

Fired up by this discussion and determined to get as straightforwardly as possible to the bottom of his current problem, Steve went home and, as he lay down to sleep he entered a meditative state in which he surrounded himself with light energy and positive forces. Just before dropping off to sleep he saw himself holding a box which represented himself. He opened it to find it filled with thick, sticky dirt which he proceeded to clean out until the box was thoroughly clean and shiny.

Then he fell asleep, only to find himself "awake" in his bedroom but, as frequently happens in lucid dreams, the room had a left/right reversal. He lay in bed and heard the door opening downstairs. Someone came toward the stairs and began to ascend. He found himself filled with fear, with an almost overwhelming terror which rose in waves from his solar plexus to his throat, never coming out in screams. As the footsteps ascended on the stairs, he became more and more fearful until finally they reached the top landing and he heard his mother's voice call out, "_____, is that you?"

In the dream reality he had a sudden knowledge of who the person was and why the reason for his fear.

Upon awaking he retained a clear memory of the dream and its preceding meditation. Within one night's time he had discovered and overcome almost completely the root cause of a problem which had been plaguing him since childhood. The symbolic messages were as clear and direct as they possibly could be. Though this particular dreamer returned to dreams of a more ordinarily symbolic nature, this experience set a plateau for his dream experiences.

The other example of changing types of dreaming also came as a dramatic result of a dream workshop. The dreamer was one who was invited to participate in the workshop because he had been having a particularly terrifying series of dreams in which he was pursued and tortured until he was almost afraid of going to sleep at night. Though he was quite familiar with dreams and dream techniques, none of them seemed to have any effect on the nightly visits from the dream marauders.

During the workshop the subject of lucid dreaming came up and this man particularly opposed the whole idea of lucid dreaming, pointing out that he felt like it was tampering with the dream state and the dream's natural message. When it was pointed out to him, however, that particularly as he already intellectually believed that minds are not divided into conscious, subconscious and a particularly hidden unconscious, but that all knowledge is available from various states in a spectrum of consciousness, it was illogical for him to believe that the dream territory was one over which he had no control and furthermore should not control, he admitted that it might be worth trying to see what he could do about controlling his dreams.

That same evening he had the following lucid dream:

> I woke up in my bedroom. It was dark with only the
> streetlight shining in. I was aware that I was dreaming.
> I went out through the wall of the bedroom. There was
> a man (one of the marauders) standing in the alley
> behind my house. I looked at him and he looked at me. I
> was afraid and came back inside. I could see through the
> wall, but he couldn't come in.
> I awoke to dawn breaking, filled with peace.

Another rather humorous dream, signifying a change in states
of awareness, was told at a dream workshop by one of the psychics
who works with the institute.

> I dreamed, she said, that every night I, and some-
> times some of my friends, would visit another country.
> This was a forbidden country and there was a fence
> between it and the country where I lived.
> But no one ever hurt me in the country I visited and
> I even made friends there.
> One night when I visited the other country some of
> friends told me I should not come the next night be-
> cause there was going to be an invasion.
> An invasion? I protested. Yes, *you* always visit our
> country but we never visit yours. Tomorrow night there
> will be an invasion. And there was.

After this dream the individual never again dreamed of visiting the foreign country but she began to exhibit her rather consid-
erable psychic talents, indeed an invasion from the psychic world
she had separated from her "ordinary" world.

In the three dreams discussed here, the switch from one type of
dreaming to another, or from one state to another, has been made
in a very rapid and somewhat dramatic manner. These dreams are
good for the purpose of illustration, and yet most people, if I am to
believe many who discuss their dreams with me, do not make rapid
and dramatic changes in their dream patterns or clarity, but rather
the dreams grow slowly as the body grows or a tree grows.

Later in this book, just as an example, I will go over a week of
my own dreams so it is possible to view the variety of dream events
that can appear in just one week and how to approach some
difficult tangles.

Chapter Six

Dreams And The Creative Self

    I had already graduated from college before I discovered that many of the authors and artists about whom I studied in my English and history and humanities courses were either extremely psychic or dreamed dreams significant to their creativity. I assume that this same discovery may have been made by others and perhaps accepted matter-of-factly; but for me the discovery was annoying and irritating in the extreme, that something which was as important as these dreams seemed to be was left out of my school textbooks; and that the picture I had been expected to accept of these authors and artists was as bloodless and sexless as the very teachers themselves seemed to be, while in reality the creators lived in a world sometimes tormented and anguished by, but certainly enlivened by dreams, nightmares, and psychic experiences of all kinds.

    The artists of our society, quite unlike the traditional school teacher's picture of them, had to be the more open-minded and open to experience; perhaps because in order to write or paint or create something one must first have experienced it—or conversely, once having experienced something one is drawn irretrievably to use it as the matter for creation.

    At any rate, once I had time to select my own reading matter I discovered a whole world of creative artists who had been spurred on by their dreams and experiences.

    There is no way, in one chapter, to record the variety and depth of dream experiences used for creative purposes, but certainly a beginning can be made.

    In the psychic readings given for their book *Creativity and the*

Intuitive Process, psychics Ellen Andrews-Negus and Stefan Grunwald claim that the creative process and the psychic process are one and the same:

"Consciousness itself and in its total form, is constantly in motion. It is an energy expressed differently in the various reality systems; but that which is expressed by your term *motion*, or *movement*, or even change is known in all reality systems. It is a part of another concept which is common to all systems, and that is creativity. They work together and in conjunction with each other—that consciousness playfully turns inward, outward, and about itself." (Reading #1477-4, Ellen Andrews-Negus for Poseidia Institute. Hindu religion expresses this concept in the form of the dancing god Shiva.)

"Your own creative abilities develop in accord with your beliefs about yourself. There are truly no real, unchanging predispositions for any lifetime. You can draw on the experience of any individual, for you are all part of a group consciousness. (You) can express sensitivity in counseling, in so-called psychic work...in art work, and so forth. We would like to make a distinction here that trance information and conscious information are truly not realistic distinctions or separations. They merely reflect the depth of focus of concentration. And to say that a trance reading is unconscious or not conscious is quite illogical, for there is nothing which is not conscious. There is no state which is not conscious.... One state is not better than another. One state is not safer than another. It simply follows your own belief as to how you choose to work." (Reading for Psychic Development Class, Ellen Andrews-Negus, December, 1977.)

Keeping these statements in mind, it is interesting and revealing to notice the number of well-known creative artists who have openly discussed their use of the dream state and other altered states of consciousness to enhance and explore their creative work.

Probably the best known literary products of the dream state are Samuel Taylor Coleridge's famous poem, *Kubla Khan*, written in 1798, and the ever-popular *Frankenstein*, the story of the first animated synthetic man, written by Mary Shelley.

Both grew directly from the dream state. Coleridge who, in somewhat desperate straits at the time, fell asleep in a chair over *Purchas's Pilgrimage* at the lines, "Here the Khan Kubla commanded a palace to be built, and a stately garden thereunto; And thus ten miles of fertile ground were enclosed within a wall," straightaway dreamed not only the scene, but the lines to the poem itself.

As he recounts in an edition of the poem published in 1816, he awoke and began to write. Partway through the writing, a knock came at the door. It was a bill collector; and by the time this unfortunate reminder of Coleridge's plight had disappeared, frustratingly, so had the remainder of his poem.

Mary Shelley, who in the company of her equally famous husband Percy Shelley, Lord Byron, and others had been reading aloud a collection of German ghost stories became part of a plan, suggested by Lord Byron, that they all write ghost stories of their own. (Interestingly enough, none of the others in the group wrote stories which were particularly noteworthy, though Byron's unfinished attempt, published in 1819, is thought to be the source of inspiration for another thriller, Bram Stoker's *Dracula*.)

According to Mary Shelley's journal of April 1817, after listening to a long conversation between Byron and Shelley on the speculation that, "Perhaps a corpse would be reanimated," she retired to her bed well after midnight where, stimulated by the evening's conversation, she could not sleep but, "My imagination, unbidden, possessed and guided me, gifting the successive images that arose in my mind with a vividness far beyond the usual bounds of reverie," and thereupon came the vision of *Frankenstein*. Guided by the idea that what frightened her would frighten other people and encouraged by her husband to expand the tale from its original few pages, she finished the book by the end of the next year.

Some of the best known authors of that genre of literature known as the children's story, those books which we read as children and live to read again as adults and read to our own children, have also been familiar friends with the dream world: C.S. Lewis, Lewis Carroll, Robert Louis Stevenson, J.R.R. Tolkien, to name just a few.

Robert Louis Stevenson recounts in his "Chapter on Dreams" in the volume of essays *Across the Plains* that often he was aided in the dream state by what he calls "the Little People" or "Brownies."

In time of need, Stevenson said, when he was stuck with a plot or didn't know how the story would come out, these "Little People" would help him out, often by telling him a story piecemeal in the dream state so that he himself would not know the outcome.

After worrying for several days, Stevenson says, he once dreamed three scenes of "Dr Jekyll" which became central to one of his most famous works, *Dr. Jekyll and Mr. Hyde*.

J.R.R. Tolkien, the eminently popular author of *The Hobbit* and a famous ring-cycle trilogy *The Lord of the Rings*, felt so strongly about the connections and the distinctions between the fairy tales he made so popular and dreams or work resulting from dreams, that he commented in his essay "On Fairy-Stories," published in *The Tolkien Reader* that:

"I would also exclude (as a fairy-story) any story that uses the machinery of Dream, the dreaming of actual human sleep, to explain the apparent occurrence of its marvels. At the least, even if the reported dream was in other respects in itself a fairy-story, I would condemn the whole as gravely defective: like a good picture in a disfiguring frame. It is true that Dream is not unconnected with Faerie. In dreams strange powers of the mind may be unlocked. In some of them a man may for a space wield the power of Faerie, that power which even as it conceives the story, causes it to take living form and colour before the eyes. A real dream may indeed sometimes be a fairy-story of almost elvish ease and skill— while it is being dreamed. But if a waking writer tells you that a tale is only a thing imagined in his sleep, he cheats deliberately the primal desire at the heart of Faerie: the realization, independent of the conceiving mind, of imagined wonder."

Tolkien goes on to say in the same essay that: "The tale itself may, of course, be so good that one cannot ignore the frame. Or it may be successful and amusing as a dream-story. So are Lewis Carroll's "Alice" stories, with their dream-frame and dream-transitions. For this (and other reasons) they are not fairy-stories."

It is far from the purpose of this book to make such esoteric distinctions as the one Tolkien draws between the fairy-story and the dream-story, but it must be seen that the dream state has earned sufficient recognition from a large number of artists that it cannot be denied its place either as an impetus or a result of artistic work.

It is interesting to note that the author of another ring-cycle, and one with which Tolkien claims his little tale of Frodo and Bilbo Baggins has no connection, Richard Wagner, also dreamed. Wagner spoke often of the blissful dream state into which he fell while composing, and wrote in a letter to a friend that the opening to his *Das Rheingold* came to him while he lay half-asleep on a sofa in a hotel in Spezia.

Tolkien's ring story, which came at the outbreak of World War II, depicts the triumph of valor and humility over the forces of darkness. Wagner's famous work was, in many ways, the clarion call for the German master race.

Another famous German, Nobel Prize-winning author Herman Hesse, also recognized the importance of dreams throughout his long writing career. *Demian*, the most popular of his early works (which also bespoke the outbreak of World War II), carries a dreamlike quality throughout, and the author's pacifist and anti-Nazi sentiments are portrayed in the book's central figure, Sinclair.

Probably one of the most important dream scenes in all of literature is portrayed in Hesse's novel *Steppenwolf* when, looking for his *anima*, Hermine, at the Masked Ball, Harry Haller enters into a somnabulistic world in which he sees the sign reading

"TONIGHT AT THE MAGIC THEATRE. FOR MAD MEN
ONLY. PRICE OF ADMITTANCE YOUR MIND. NOT FOR
EVERYBODY. HERMINE IS IN HELL."

Hesse spent several months in therapy with Carl Jung, an
event which not only dramatically altered the course of his writing
career, but was forever to impress upon him the importance of the
dream world and the world of metaphysics.

Certainly, however, the world of dreams has not claimed only
those artists with as strongly developed a sense of the mystical as
Hesse, Stevenson and Tolkien. One of America's most down-to-
earth and practical as well as representatively popular authors, the
beloved Mark Twain, also gave credence to the inspiration of
dreams, and with good reason: he was often the dreamer of precognitive dreams. One of these came true in a tragic way, as told by
Samuel Clemens to his official biographer, Albert Bigelow Paine.

One night Clemens, who was then a junior pilot on the
Mississippi River steamboat *Pennsylvania*, dreamed about his
younger brother Henry, of whom he was very fond.

In 1858 Sam had been able to secure for Henry a position as
clerk on the *Pennsylvania* and the two had great times together.

On the night of the dream, the *Pennsylvania* tied up at St.
Louis. Sam spent the night with his sister Pamela who lived in that
city. Clemens reported that in the dream he found himself in the
sitting room of his sister's house. Resting on two chairs was a metal
coffin. Looking inside, Clemens found the body of his brother
Henry with a bouquet of white flowers, a crimson rose in its center,
lying on his chest.

When Clemens awoke the next morning, the dream as is often
the case, seemed so real that he believed it to be true. He thought he
would go downstairs and take one last look at his brother's face;
but then, changing his mind, went out for a walk. It was not until
Twain reached the middle of the block that he realized he had been
dreaming. He ran back to the house in a state of joy, told his sister
the dream and then seemingly forgot about it.

In the meantime there was friction on the boat and Sam left his
job to go aboard another steamer, the *Lacey*. Henry remained on
the *Pennsylvania* as clerk.

Clemens remembered that the night before the *Pennsylvania*
started up river, the first time they were apart, he gave his brother
some advice about what to do in case of a river accident. Two days
later, the *Lacey* touched in at the port of Greenville, Mississippi,
only to hear from the wharf, "The *Pennsylvania* is blown up just
below Memphis at Ship Island! One hundred and fifty lives lost!"

Althought it was hoped that Henry Clemens would recover
from the burns he sustained in the fire, he died six days after the

explosion in an improvised hospital in Memphis. Most of the victims of the disaster were laid out in plain pinewood coffins; but for Henry, whose handsome features had particularly attracted the attention of the Memphis ladies, a collection had been taken up to purchase a metal coffin.

When Clemens walked into the room everything was as it had been in his dream with the exception of one detail. As Sam Clemens stood looking at his brother's body an elderly woman walked into the room carrying a bouquet of white flowers at the center of which was one crimson rose. She laid it on Henry's breast.

Twain never wrote particularly about dreams or spoke of them in his famous, humorous lectures, but he was plagued and entranced throughout his entire adult life by dreams of a certain lovely female to whom he felt extraordinarily close. Sometimes she would appear in the costume of one time period, sometimes another, but always the same lovely face. He never found her in waking life.

Though most of the artists spoken of here are literary figures, and indeed perhaps it is more common for the writer to describe his dream events for publication than any other type of creator, certainly writers are not the only persons to receive creative inspiration from dreams. The list goes on and on, and there are far more stories of dreams than there is room to tell them.

Author George Sand recounts, for example, of her tempestuous and emotion-filled affair with the composer Frederic Chopin that when he went with her and her two children to the Balearic Islands in 1838, one of his most famous pieces of music, the B-minor Prelude, resulted from a troubled dream.

Traveling to rouse himself from morbid, feverish depression, Chopin spent long hours in Majorca at the piano. One day the novelist Sand, and her son, Maurice, away from home were overtaken and delayed by a storm. They arrived home to find Chopin at the piano composing the B-minor Prelude. Rising with a cry, he looked at the storm-beaten pair, "Ah! I knew well you were dead!" He had dreamed that he saw himself "drowned in a lake; heavy, cold drops of water fell at regular intervals" on his breast.

Quite fortunately for all of us, the usefulness of dreams toward the creative process does not end with the very famous, but can be equally helpful to the struggling artist or the ordinary individual who wants to explore creativity, which is a gift to all of us.

It is to this that I wish to devote this chapter, hoping that it might inspire public school teachers, such as I have been, or other persons to whom young people look for guidance to allow some of the dream-inspired creativity to become an ordinary part of life. I would like to recount one of my own experiences.

When I began teaching writing classes at a Virginia Beach high school in 1973, I had no real idea of developing my own techniques for teaching writing. What I did know was that I enjoyed teaching writing more than anything else, because it seemed to me to be one of the few places in which the public school system made allowance for natural creativity.

What happened the day I walked into the first high school writing class was a surprise even to me. I gave the assignment which I had intended as a loosening-up technique, something geared to teach the fact that true creativity comes from within: "Write a dream," I said, "a dream you've had recently, or one you remember from your childhood. Write an interpretation of the dream, and then write a short story from it."

It was if I'd said the magic word. When I said the word dream, a dozen bored faces came alive. "You know how to interpret dreams?" one girl said.

"What does it mean when you sleepwalk?" another asked.

"What does it mean when you dream you were someplace and your friend dreams he was the same place and you both remember it?"

The class began an adventure into the exploration of the unconscious mind that intrigued one group of students after another for the three years I taught in Virginia public schools and continues for some of them even now. It produced that year the second-place award-winning short story in the state student writing competition, and two years later both the first-place short story and first and third place poems in the same contest.

What happened? It is my belief that something in the magic of the class unleashed the creativity of some extraordinary and even very ordinary students.

It started, naturally, from my own interest in writing. No subject, I believe, can be taught effectively by someone who performs the act of teaching as rote exercise without enjoyment of the subject itself, and I had loved writing from the time I could first hold a pencil.

Yet an interest in writing was certainly not the only thing that sparked the first class or the classes after it. I had been teaching writing off and on since the first teaching job I took the year after I graduated from college. Quite probably my maturing understanding of people and their individual problems played a part, since I was more willing to help the students learn to let the words flow freely from their minds to the paper without having to judge them. Yet there was something else.

Drawn, almost unwillingly, from that first class session into subject areas that I knew from past experience could "get me in trouble" in the ordinary teaching world, I began very cautiously to explore the depths of a knowledge for which these young people did not even have a vocabulary, but which they surely possessed.

I moved very cautiously at first, already concerned with the disapproving look I had received from the vice-principal when I told her I was involved with an organization which studied psychics, yet feeling pushed by the questions my students began bringing me daily about their dreams. They even began bringing their friends around between classes for lessons in how to interpret their dream symbols. I pushed caution aside and devoted one class exclusively to understanding how to interpret dream symbology, pointing out to them how writers down through the ages have drawn on the same universal symbols to develop allegory and fiction which has struck chords deep in our souls. The dream teaching spilled over into my regular English classes at the request of students there, making the teaching of fiction and poetry more of a challenge and less of a chore.

One day early in the Fall, one of the writing class students, a pale, shy girl named Christie who was living through the breakup of her parents' marriage, came into the classroom early as I was hurrying to correct some papers.

"God spoke to me for the third time last night," she said confidentially as she walked up to my desk.

Trying not to look too surprised, I asked in the same manner, "Oh, what happened?"

She proceeded to report a dream in which she found herself atop a large cross. "On the first day, there was nothing," she said, "nothing, just gray. On the second day there was a huge storm, thunder and lightning and huge waves. On the third day, the sun came out and God spoke to me and He said, 'You have done good.'"

From her hushed tones it was obvious to see that she had had what one might call a mystical experience. Life had been tough for this girl. From what was apparently a fairly strong Christian upbringing she had lived through having her mother walk away, the remarriage of her father to a woman whose morals she could not condone, and having to care for a fairly large group of younger brothers and sisters, step-brothers and step-sisters.

I hesitated to ask her what God has said to her the other two times He talked to her, but said, "Why don't you write about it?" as the rest of the class was coming in. She wrote a poem of great beauty and maturity which I wish to this day I had kept since she dropped out of school soon after that and I lost contact with her.

And Christie was not the only one whose writing seemed to grow as the members of this class were allowed a chance to explore their thoughts and abilities.

In an earlier chapter I told the story of Susan, the cheerleader, whose grandmother had died. In the five years since her grandmother's death, the experience had obviously run like an undercurrent in this girl's life, unheeded by her parents or any of the others around her. It was to her grandmother that Susan often took her concerns under the guise of dreams, yet obviously the question nagged at her as to whether this was a "sane" thing to do.

When her question about whether any of the others ever dreamed about anyone who had died was received by her peers not with scorn but with sympathy and interest she obviously took comfort from it.

Asked to write a story about her experiences, she produced a rather magical little children's tale about a little girl whose grandmother kept an eye on her even though death had separated them. Once again, here was a young person who made rather ordinary grades, who did not come to the class with any particular writing ability, but had taken it because it was not a science class and fit into her busy senior schedule. The amount of creativity in the story was attested to by the warm response it received from other students.

Some of the stories they wrote had an obvious science fiction quality as they began to explore their own experiences with time. The boy who asked, "What does it mean when you and your friend both dream you are at the same place at the same time and you both remember it?" had had a personal experience with non-linear time which led him to explore the subject even further.

After some of the class members had experienced lucid dreaming (which they accomplished with a rapidity even I found alarming after knowing adults who had spent months with no success) one of the girls announced to the class a problem which has puzzled philosophers for centuries:

"If David is at home and I call him," she said, "he exists; but sometimes if David is at home and I don't call him, he doesn't exist."

Egged on by this outrageous statement, the class (including David) gave her argument after argument while I listened with growing amusement. Finally, in what appeared to be anger, she got up, walked out and slammed the door behind her.

I always tried to give my class as much freedom as possible without disrupting anything in the rest of the school, so I let her go, thinking it would be good to have a cooling-off period. We went on with a discussion of other matters until almost the end of the period. Attention shifted and everyone, including myself, forgot about this girl and her exit. About one minute before the bell rang for class change the door opened again. We all looked up from our discussion. There stood our recalcitrant class member with a mischievious grin on her face. Dramatically she paused in the doorway. "See, I didn't exist, did I?" she announced to a round of laughter and applause.

If a tree falls in the forest without anyone to see or hear it, has it really fallen? What teacher has not been delighted when a student comes up with a fresh-faced discovery unaware that textbooks have discussed it for years?

The question of time was not so easily dismissed, however, by a few of this group. One boy, Steve, had dreamed repeatedly as a child about lying in the bottom of a boat watching the bank go by on either side.

Though he lived near the water all his life, he had no conscious recall of an experience to match this one until he was much older. In the first "write a dream" experience, I encouraged him to explore this dream extending the travel in his imagination until the boat reached its destination.

By the time he finished this exploration I was confronted by a student who insisted that the child in the boat was not Steve as he knew himself today, but another boy, Joshua, who lived in frontier America and was escaping from the Indians. Was there, he asked me, really such a thing as reincarnation?

How can we argue with someone's experience? I find that I can argue all I want that something did not happen or that the facts were really different, but people's perceptions seldom change.

I told him what I knew about reincarnation and led him to some books on the subject feeling that at any moment I might get expelled myself for teaching inflammatory subjects. (Even though while teaching my American Literature classes, I found it very hard to teach Transcendentalism without approaching the question of reincarnation, which was already known to some.)

The adventure for Steve did not end there. A serious student of any subject which interested him, he began to ask questions about symbolism, about yoga, about meditation. One day he came to class asking whether anyone ever heard voices.

Asleep in his room for an after-school nap, he said, he had heard the telephone ring and had tried to answer it but no one was there. This event recurred. Then going back to sleep, he heard someone calling his name. He thought it was his younger brother, but going dowstairs, he discovered that he had been alone in the house and that his little brother, who was just coming in the door from school, had not called him.

Not long after this incident, he came to me before class and said in an urgent tone, "I really have to talk to you." I invited him to stay after class a few minutes since I had a free period.

The story which unfolded would have made anyone a little nervous. On a class field trip that weekend, Steve said, he had been riding on a bus crowded with other students and since he hadn't had much sleep he decided to try to meditate and clear his mind. Almost immediately, he said, he found himself swimming in the ocean (in fact he was a strong swimmer and this was an oceanography field trip) talking, or being talked to, by a porpoise who called himself Thonar. The porpoise explained why, as an intelligence, porpoises had left the land and many other things.

"If I told this to anybody," Steve said (telling it to me), "they'd think I was nuts!"

Well, I am sorry to say, he was probably right. His experiences of extraordinary phenomena had by that time so transcended the experiences of his contemporaries that had he explained them even to a school psychiatrist (or perhaps particularly to a school psychiatrist) he might have been carefully examined and an attempt made to persuade him to drop his delusions. However, he did not seem to be attempting to use his experiences to compensate for any other lack in his life so I agreed to keep his experiences confidential.

In the meantime he went on to write a prize-winning short story incorporating something of what he had learned about symbology.

I must add that in the case of some of the other students who came to me, I was not so confident of their ability to handle their dreams without help. As a teacher I could go only so far in taking time to help individuals understand their problems, and when one of the girls in writing class brought a friend who had been consistently dreaming vampire dreams both where he was pursued by vampires and where he himself became a vampire, I recommended that he contact the best counselor I knew for an intensive examination of his attitude toward himself and others.

When school was almost over that year, some of the students began to say that they didn't want the class to be over, and asked me to go on teaching them over the summer. I laughed at the compliment, thinking it was a piece of nostalgic madness that sometimes gets into students at the end of a school year. And finally, to humor them, agreed that if they would appear at my house at a particular day and time, I'd teach a summer writing class. I expected they would forget about it when school was over.

Instead, ten students showed up at the appointed time. Others sent word that they were sorry they couldn't make it, but summer jobs were keeping them away.

Feeling surprised and honored, I began then seriously to think about developing techniques for teaching writing which extended beyond the methods by which I myself had been taught. I used some techniques such as the very effective one taught me by a high school writing teacher of my own, stream of consciousness. This writing warm-up exercise consisted solely of having the student spend the first ten or fifteen minutes of a class period writing as quickly as they could anything and everything that came into their minds, censoring as little as possible. Much like what happens in a dream, the result was a loosening of the censorship that beginning writers so often put on their writing, wanting it to meet standards they have been taught are right and proper. Many of my students began to use this technique quite effectively anytime they sat down to write, even themes and papers for other classes.

I had thrown out almost immediately the standardized text-book which had been ordered for my school classes because it used what is a fairly common workbook method of imitating the styles of other writers—not that I considered it unimportant to read other writers and their styles; but it had always struck me as incongruous that anyone could learn to create while attempting to imitate the style of someone else, especially that style represented by brief excerpts from much longer works.

So I began to devise techniques for writing through under-standing the creative self. The techniques I used that summer included writing from the perspective of various objects in the house, writing from the perspective of the plants, writing about experiences of early childhood and always reading the work aloud, reading each other's work aloud, commenting on it, talking about it.

Beginning writers are usually frightened of the blank sheet of paper before them. They are frightened of the opinions of others about their writing, and they are frightened of making mistakes. Yet unconsciously, when speaking, they will use language musi-cally and expressively. The trick is to get them to unblock the fear of turning language into words crystallized on paper.

Since this is a book about dreaming, not one about writing, I will not list all of the techniques my young dreamers encouraged me to develop. One of the nice writing techniques certainly, and one that is expressed so beautifully by Hermann Hesse at the end of his novel *The Glass Bead Game (Magister Ludi)*, is that of having the students choose another time and place with which they feel comfortable and familiar, and write themselves into it. By the time I tried this approach that summer, I was already working with people who believed in reincarnation as a fact and who were using their dreams and other experiences to explore time and space; but I have since used it quite effectively with people who do not believe in reincarnation and I don't think it makes much difference. What a wonderful and exciting way it would also be to teach history.

I was not too surprised when I returned to school the next Fall to find another group of writing students as interesting and as interested as the first. Coming from a broad range of backgrounds extending from very conservative Christian to very agnostic to Zen Buddhism, the group used characters drawn from their dreams to interact with each other and explore their own feelings.

The thing that did surprise me was when those students and again the students from the year following began to become friends with one another and began to form a chain of friendship which extended far beyond graduation and even into the present; and that each year, with new additions, the group would ask for the class to go on even into the summers.

It is my opinion that there was no magic used here, no special charisma or anything of the sort. These people came to know each other and respect each other through the language of dreams—perhaps the deepest, most honest language we have. And they liked it, found it meeting a need unmet elsewhere in their world and wanted it to continue. At present these former students are college students, young business people, housewives, working mothers, and a variety of other things which cover the occupational field. The thing which they have in common and which binds them to one another is their continuing interest in dreams and creativity.

One last amusing incident, and one whose creativity cannot be denied is that of Joe Fredd. Joe Fredd was the creation of one of the students as the result of the first dream assignment, obviously an alter ego. In the assignment which asked the students to allow their characters to interact, Joe Fredd interacted with the characters of many of the students in the class—an alternately awkward and suave ladies' man.

As the class went on, Joe Fredd took on a life of his own. Through his mischevious creators, he obtained a library card, signed hall passes, took exams and traveled to other classes. He became known to half the senior class.

Today, several years later, Joe Fredd still exists and occasionally via letter or word-of-mouth I hear of his exploits. I hope he never dies.

Chapter Seven

Healing With Dreams

The question of whether dreams can be used for healing purposes is one that has intrigued many people throughout the ages. The Bible, folklore, and other recorded elements of history recount many instances of the power of dreams, such as Joseph's precognitive awareness of famine and pestilence in Egypt and his ability to convince the pharoah to prepare for same. Yet the question of whether dreams can be used for actual healing purposes remains.

Earlier we talked about using dreams for the practical purposes of healing oneself—the dream which warned of improper diet, the need for more or different exercise, an upcoming illness or accident which could be averted.

Surely in this sense dreams can be used for healing purposes and are—often without the dreamer himself being aware of it since science seems to show that dreaming itself is necessary for health and the dream-deprived person can incur serious illness.

However the question posed here is on an even broader scale than whether an individual can use his or her own dreams for healing purposes; can dreams be used for the purpose of healing someone else?

The tales in the early Christian church of saints coming in the form of dream or vision for the purpose of healing are almost too numerous to mention. And there certainly does seem to be the propensity for some particularly talented dreamers to select the destination of their dreaming and unerringly attend to some chosen task.

Joan Grant, whom I mentioned earlier as particularly talented in the recall of other life experiences, seems to have been one of these types of dreamers. And in her voluminous writings, particularly her autobiographical work *Far Memory* and the book *Many Lifetimes*, which she co-authored with psychiatrist Denys Kalsey, she tells of instances where she, while at home in bed dreaming, would be seen in the sickrooms of friends, chatting with them, calming them before operations and so on.

As a child during World War I this same Joan Grant, whose parents kept from her any word of the war going on because they felt she was too young to be exposed to its horrors, used to dream of soldiers wounded at the front and going there to help them. Thinking she was mad, she only later discovered the accuracy of these dreams when she accurately told a cousin the names of certain commanders at the front.

This sort of activity is apparently not as uncommon as one might think from reports of groups taking dream seminars and classes. One of my students spent several months of what she called "lucid dreaming practice," going various places to help people. On one occasion, she said, it was an old alcoholic wandering about in a semi-conscious state whom she took to "friends" and asked them to take care of him. In another case she made visits to a young girl who was incarcerated in the mental ward of a city hospital. The girl was near catatonia and the two conversed telepathically about the girl's condition, which improved.

Naturally it would be possible to dismiss such experiences more easily in the case of the student who had no verifiable evidence that her experience was anything more than symbolic. The catatonic girl and the alcoholic man could have represented certain aspects of her personality which she needed to examine. And, of course, there is a certain amount of validity to that opinion since, as previously stated, it appears that we never dream anything at any time, or for that matter have any waking experience, that does not have some meaning symbolic to our personality.

And yet there are certainly cases other than Joan Grant's and those of my student which seem to imply that the dream state can be used by one person to aid in the healing of another.

When I first moved to Virginia Beach I met a woman—let us call her Andrea—who had a veritable hospital (in fact, that is what her friends called it), where at night she would work with individuals who asked her for help.

In the daytime Andrea, a rather ordinary mother of three or four grown children, had returned to college to finish a graduate degree in psychology. At first she kept quiet about her interests but finally found her professors so interested that she began to talk and even submitted to a variety of psychological tests—which proved she was normal. She had no medical training.

Two people with whom I was familiar went to Andrea with medical problems, one had a severe case of *herpes*, the other a tumor which doctors wanted to remove for fear of malignancy. In both cases the patients went to Andrea asking to be admitted to her "hospital." Andrea, who seldom talked about her abilities, admitted when questioned that she was often quite aware of the patient's existence in her dream reality and would administer to her patients either at their homes or in her dream hospital.

In the case of the *herpes*, the individual seemed to show improvement until he again began to produce the conditions which had created the disease itself. In the second case, the case of the tumor, the patient recovered completely. In addition to nightly treatments in the "hospital," Andrea treated her patient regularly in the waking world with a method known in religious communities as "laying on of hands." The primary modern definition of the method used by "holy" persons throughout the ages, is that "the spirit" or God directs energy through the healer to the patient or the individual being healed.

This type of faith healing is regaining a widespread popularity today through the auspices of such individuals as Ruth Carter Stapleton, American President Jimmy Carter's evangelical sister, and other practitioners such as born-again Christians and members of the Charismatic Catholic movement.

Examined by the same doctors who planned to perform surgery, the woman who had daily seen the disintegration of her tumorous growth was told her recovery was strange and miraculous. She did not inform them of her unorthodox treatment.

Another man, a Boston-bred healer who worked with Poseidia Institute for a time, came to me one day with the question, "Do you think it's possible to heal people from the dream state?" I asked him why the question.

The previous night, he said, his wife had been experiencing a severe pain in her leg. He had done what he could using ordinary relaxation techniques and then had himself gone to sleep.

During the night he had the following dream experience. He was examining his wife's leg, looking at it almost as if he had X-ray vision. Once having located the source of the pain, he said, it was as if he was seeing balls of energy, points of light which worked upon the pain until it disappeared. When he awoke, his wife was feeling fine.

There was no doubt in my mind that this man had a healing ability. Always relatively humble and questioning, he told the story of his first healing experience which happened among dozens of witnesses. He had been attending a conference on healing where participants were taught and allowed to practice healing techniques on one another.

At one point in the conference a woman had taken the role of patient while my friend played the role of healer. When he finished she said she felt much better, and since it was lunchtime he suggested that they go get some lunch together.

As they walked down the drive together talking, he noticed that they were being followed by a women in a car but did not give it much thought until they arrived at the restaurant, a short walk away. The driver of the car was the woman's sister who arrived with tears of joy on her face. It seems that the patient had for some time suffered from a debilitating heart disease and for years had not been able to walk more than a few steps without assistance.

The American Indians have always believed in the healing power of dreams and one of the best-known Indian historical figures is Black Elk, an Oglala Sioux immortalized by prize-winning author John Neihardt.

When Black Elk was nine years old, he said, he became ill with a sickness that started with a weakening of his legs and then his entire body became swollen and puffy. At first, when the tribe was moving, he was carried in a pony drag; and finally, when the tribe camped again, he was sick in his family tepee. For twelve long days and nights he lay in a delirium and was not expected to live.

It was during this time that Black Elk had his greatest vision of his tribe and one which would sustain him for the rest of his life. During this vision he perceived himself to be in his body, but his legs did not hurt him and his body was very light. In his vision Black Elk saw the Powers of the World. These Powers imparted their powers to him and he saw the history of the hoop of the Indian nations, an event which led him to visionary historical predictions throughout his lifetime. Finally, his vision completed, he found himself alone on a broad plain. He could see his family's village far ahead and began to walk toward it, finally entering his own tepee where he saw his parents bending over a sick boy who was himself. Someone was saying, "The boy is coming to, you'd better give him some water."

In typical Indian tradition, Black Elk had been attended by the tribal medicine man, Whirlwind Chaser, and Black Elk's parents insisted that it had been Whirlwind Chaser who effected the cure. The medicine man was given the family's best horse and there was much talk about his power and ability.

"I knew it was the Grandfathers in the Flaming Rainbow Tepee (of his vision) who had cured me," Black Elk is quoted as saying, "but I felt afraid to say so."

And this brings us to the important question of who does the curing. Is it the healer, the doctor, the surgeon, the medicine man? Or is it the patient? Ordinarily our answer would be, as it was in the case of Black Elk's parents, the medicine man.

Yet, according to Black Elk's insistence, it was the curative power of the dream itself that made him well.

And here again, the question of time, space and reality creation rears its head. If indeed reality, all reality, is a symbolic creation of our thoughts and feelings, is it ever possible to cure someone else—or make them sick?

This became a very central question in some research work jointly carried out by the A.R.E., the Association for Research and Enlightenment, in Virginia Beach, and Poseidia Institute.

The A.R.E. was founded on the work of psychic Edgar Cayce and it is policy within that organization to never recommend the work of any other psychic though they occasionally become involved in research work with psychics. So it was a rather important step when psychologist Henry Reed, who was then supervisor of the dream research which is done at A.R.E. and editor of their *Sundance Community Dream Journal,* agreed to become involved with Poseidia staff and psychics in what he had already named a "dream helper" project.

The process was quite straightforward. During a given period of time the next local person who came to Poseidia Institute requesting a psychic reading would be offered the bonus of becoming involved in the dream helper project.

This meant that, as well as the requested psychic reading, the individual would receive pre-session and post-session counseling with one of PI's psychologists; would meet with a dream team composed of seven members of the combined A.R.E. and PI staffs for at least two sessions of "dream helper" work; and that psychic readings as well would be done on the dream helper process.

The purpose of the experiment was twofold: one, to determine whether persons other than the target individual could "dream for" that individual for the purpose of aiding in healing; and two, to determine whether these dream helpers could intuit what the target individual's problem was without verbal assistance.

Once the individual, a young college girl, was selected the dream team met with her one evening for meditation. Introductions were made (some of the dream team members were also previously unacquainted) and the group meditated together for a brief period of time. Each member of the group was then asked to go home, write down any intuitive impressions of the target individual and then record whatever dreams came during the night's sleep. The next day being Saturday, the group would again meet and discuss their dreams and impressions.

Prior to dreaming at all, out of the seven dream helpers, five picked up that the problem involved a trauma or risk (the other two dream helpers recorded no intuitive feelings). Four felt that this trauma had to do with difficulties in the pelvic area and two saw this as having to do with children or the loss of a child.

The group was later to discover that the girl was facing a traumatic conflict of involvement with an older married man, about which her family knew nothing and would certainly not approve; that she had indeed been experiencing difficulties with her reproductive organs for which she had been seeing a physician; and that earlier, while still in high school, she had experienced a traumatic abortion which very few people were aware of outside of her immediate family (including the man in question). Bear in mind then that, even before hearing the dreams, the girl found herself somewhat surprised by the intuitive impressions the group put forth.

During their discussion of the dreams (which were too numerous to report here in full), the dream team members found that their dreams centered around several themes which included: 1) cars with broken engines, 2) fires or explosions, 3) earthquakes or earth splits, 4) foreign objects, 5) other dream team members, 6) children at play or young people, and 7) energy in a circular motion. As the discussion of the dreams proceeded, the dream team members also discovered that there were certain philosophical and emotional conflicts between them which were stimulated by the target individual's problems and depicted in the dreams.

Some examples of the dream team's dreams were:

Dream 1. We as a group (the dream team) were all riding around a roller rink on children's tricycles, very awkwardly manipulating and colliding with each other.

Dream 2. I am inside a house with the dream helpers group. We hear loud explosions outside, so I lift the curtain and look to the east. Black smoke is rising into the sky. It seems that a boat has exploded on a nearby canal or channel that runs through a town.

As we stand at the window looking out, I suddenly realize that we are all dreaming and that we are having a collective vision of another place in a different time. The scene is one of a city. The colors are especially vivid. My impression is that the city is on the water (the sea) because of the boat channel.

I say to the others that we are dreaming. Some of them seem in doubt, or maybe doubting that we should recognize the fact.

Dream 3. Later, this same individual dreams: A couple has invited their parents out to dinner. The older couple accepts, but only because they need to get out and get some exercise. I have a feeling of tension, that the parents are insincere or inconsiderate, and not really appreciative of the younger couple's gesture.

Dream 4. (Many dreams early in the night where I'm aware I'm in a dream helper project and it is going well.) Moving into a new house. My mother and father were also moving in. Don't have a lot of furniture but I am distributing it among the rooms.

Since I am going to be around the longest, I have been given the larger (nicer) of the bedrooms. It is in the back of the house. They have the one in the front near the street where I have usually been. I'm glad I'll be having a less noisy, more peaceful area. The prominent colors in their bedroom are light green and rose and there are full bloom roses on the bed sheets. These are the correct colors even though the sheets don't fit too well but the idea is they can get better fitting ones later. I see Mother, but Father isn't there right now. Mother is very tired and doesn't much care about the sheets, but she knows Father will complain.

I distribute the lamps so that we can see even though it's not likely we will get them hung on the walls tonight since Mother is very tired. She wants to sleep but I want to continue tonight working on the moving project. I'm not aware of any other people being in the house, but I think there are others who will be living there.

I have a nice bedroom with two double beds and nice dressers, cabinets and lamps. It seems that this is somehow connected to the dreaming project.

Dream 5. I am a young black girl about sixteen or seventeen. I am walking home from school with a friend (male) when a white man asks us to come into his house. We feel we must go because he is white and it is a small town.

Once inside we realize that the man has either committed or is going to commit a murder and blame it on us. I struggle to get away and to release the prisoner who is bound and going to be killed while the man's wife watches from a stairway.

But the man has a knife and is slicing at me while I struggle with him. I think my friend got away in the struggle. I feel the pain in my arm as the knife rips slices out of me.

Finally I do get away, I think, because the man

upturns an oil lamp on the table. There is a fire in which I know the man and his prisoner are killed anyway. I run for the door afraid of being pursued, run across the street and begin running through yards. Many of the yards have fences or hedges and there are dogs in the yards. But the dogs are chained and I avoid them and escape.

Dream 6. A group of us are traveling to a place, staying the night at a motel. There is a service station. I or we were given two cars. One is a pick-up truck that was overheating. The other is a Buick which was having trouble with its pipes. We took the Buick. Something about food choice.

From just the dreams given here it is clear to see how the dream helpers' dreams focused on explosive situations, and dreams which have to do with sexuality and parental involvement or the involvement of someone who might disapprove. The question that remains is one of whether the dreams actually connected with the target person in a way that would provide help or healing.

In order to discuss this I would like to quote from readings given by one of the psychics involved in the project, Christi Anna Davidson:

Channel: "Some of the things we want to discuss here are the nature of dreaming, the dreaming process. We want to come to a better understanding of what occurs during sleep. Not only does this process occur during sleep but it also occurs during the waking hours, although it is not very noticeable. But the mind of each individual is constantly active with the imaginative realm, at the pattern-making realm. We can, at times, tune into its various facets even while we are awake. It is from these levels of self that some of the inspiration and insight intrude. It goes hand in hand with the linear, rational mind. They are to work as cooperative partners in both times, i.e., during waking and sleeping. However, now there is usually a separation between the two, so that the imaginative mind is more active during sleep and the linear mind more active during waking. There should be much more balancing of these functions.

"Now we often get insights in dreams but this type of project has the additional effects of delving into and understanding better the experience that occurred during the dreaming, and of sharing that. This releases more energy than if any one person was doing it on their own. It also helps to bring out the oneness of mind, the overlapping of individuality, the interweaving of individuality and oneness. It is an experience at that level and it is very valuable.

Conductor: "Thank you for that opening statement. You've begun to answer some of the questions but we'll go through them so that any additions might be made.

"Discuss the theory and process of helping another person with healing through one's own dreams."

Channel: "As we have been clarifying, it is not only that we might help another person but that we might help ourselves, that we might help the totality of the group by pooling experiences and pooling our viewpoints and having the other people there help us clarify our own blockages, our own misunderstandings and open us up for our own healing.

"The target person, as was said, acts more as the person who decides what area of our overall experience will be catalyzed. Now at some level each member of the dream team is aware of the area that will be catalyzed, but that is not the most important factor here; it's rather the understanding of how the target person is like the, what you call, the lightning rod or the attractor of a particular theme and it is out of our own unselfishness that we are willing to share those parts of ourselves that relate to that theme.

"As has been said, in a dream of Christi Anna's many years ago, this is a particular time period in which much spiritual growth can be obtained through small group interaction. One of the reasons for this is to begin to show the oneness, the interconnection of mind, the interconnection of experience.

"Is there further on this question?"

Conductor: "Yes, please. Can you elucidate interconnection of mind? Can you explain that process better, more fully?"

Channel: "There is only one mind, one mass of consciousness. Mass is not exactly the right word but that will give a feeling for it. We all as individuals have access to that mind and have developed our own particular pathways into this overall mass of mind, our own little neurological pathways. However, remember that it is only a particular pathway that we are traveling and we have the choice of traveling varieties of neurological pathways in this overall brain of God and just as all experience is recorded in the individual mind, so is all experience recorded in the brain of God. And as different experiences are recorded in different areas of the brain, likewise in the brain of God.

"Now habit patterns, particular preconceptions, tend to keep us in certain grooves within that overall mind, but that overall mind is our minds and we can learn to make grooves anywhere in that mind that we choose, and just as we have instant access to our own individual brain, instantly at any particular area of it, likewise with the brain of God. It is not a question of going here, there or the other for it. It is all accessible if you choose to search for that aspect of it, if you choose to allow the impulses of that aspect of the overall brain of God to impinge on your individual self.

"So think a little more deeply about how your own individual brain works and then understand that this is very analagous to the overall workings of the mind of God. Is this clear?"

Reading #2, given May 31, 1978 by Christi Anna Davidson.

Conductor: "The next dream is, _____ is missing. She's been kidnapped. There is a feeling of ominous concern."

Channel: "Here is reflected _____'s concern about his loss of contact with creative and sexual energy, his feeling out of touch with those aspects of self; or particularly fears that they will be taken away, and that as he shows some of his cantankerous sides that he will be punished by having his creative nature absconded.

"Also here are some concerns on the dreamer's part about the state of the sexual relationship between them. Some concern about its absence. Some feelings of loss for areas in his life that are not getting enough nurturing, that are being somewhat pushed aside. There is definitely a feeling of sorrow here and it would be well for _____ and _____ to have continuing communication about this so that they increase even more their understanding of each other in this area of their sexual relationship.

"How this ties in with the target person, the target person stimulated the area of sexuality and its expression and when that topic was raised, this was the particular thought or patterns that were stirred for _____.

"I am particularly tuned in here to the deep level of sadness, sorrowing, mournfulness that is raised for _____ when this topic came up. Hopefully (as an aside here), as we go through these dreams we will be able to get a better handle on how the overall experience can be a healing one and not just a rehashing of different people's perspective. There will possibly need to be in the ceremony some aspects additional to just the sharing of the dream because, as we are seeing, so far it is bringing up the issues, awakening, stimulating them.

There needs to be a little more concern and emphasis on healing of these issues. As this particular dream project was constituted there were some lacks or lack of strength in this area. This is certainly something that needs more attention.

"It is nice to know that we can all tune in to a particular area. The people here involved generally knew that already, but there needs to be the healing, the integration, the expanding, the soothing of the area stimulated and the group can be used in better ways to promote that healing process. It is not enough to just have a particular area stirred up or catalyzed. Even though this particular step of this dream helpers project is over, there would be a way to add some of this healing in an additional step and it would be a good idea to do so. So do think about this. Next."

Conductor: "So that we may help each other better, please describe a more useful process for the dream helper ceremony."

Channel: "It would be better if the people involved, particularly the leaders of the project, put their energy into doing this. In general what is needed is more time for healing, more attention on that process. We hit the beginning of the process by our sharing but it would be the addition of group meditation with laying on of hands. It could be the giving of some type of . . . use the word gift to each member that would signify desire for oneness and healing. Some making up of each individual making up a prayer for themselves and the group and using it for several days of a week. Things that would remind each person involved that they are open to healing or growth or more attunement within the topic area. Sending of healing energies to each other and of aiming for an attitude of mind that says, 'I have just shown you my opinion. I ask for the Divine within myself to make that opinion be even more attuned to the overall divine nature. I am willing to accept any changes necessary in this area to bring more of that attunement. I am willing to be involved in the healing process.' Of course, this healing process might continue over six months, a year, but at the time of the dream helpers project there should be more of a focusing on the healing aspect so that the overall process can be augmented. That is sufficient on that for now."

These two readings, of course, are only the opinion given through one psychic of what the Dream Helper Project was about and what it could accomplish in terms of healing; yet they certainly reiterated what to me seem to be imporant concepts such as:

1. There is no healing except self-healing.
2. There is no self except that which includes all of us. Personality self is, in the final analysis, illusory.
3. We exist in what is called here "the mind of God," a timeless, spaceless universe wherein all things are available to us.
4. Working within this concept, within this approach to dreaming can only aid in the healing not only of someone who considers himself or herself to have a serious illness, but in the whole universe since we are inter-connected.
5. Projects such as this are a new and unique method of approaching the ills of the world.

I feel that something should be said about the problems of research within a structure such as the Dream Helper Project outlined here (and any other similar project). This problem was encountered almost immediately by the more scientific in the group, and it is the problem of how to statistically record and analyze the results of such work.

First of all, from the pre-dream intuitions of the dream helpers, it was obvious that many of them perceived upon first meeting, without dreaming and without conversation, some or all of what was troubling the target person. Secondly, many of the dreams seemed to center around these focal themes, and the target person seemed to be helped, but how could one ever prove it?

The answer given by the psychic to this question is one cannot prove it. Further, one cannot *prove* anything by current statistical methods, that information *is* available and that dependent on the desires of the researchers and the participants, anything could happen.

An example was given. Two dreams, it said, might talk about chairs. One of these dreams might symbolize the matter discussed in the healing project; the other might symbolize something entirely different. Later one of the directors of the project, Henry Reed, reported a conversation which he carried out with professor Robert Vandercastle of the University of Virginia's Dream Research Laboratory. The two had spoken for over half an hour about the Dream Helper Project when they realized that they had been using quite different words and that had their conversations been recorded and then analyzed by a researcher for symbolic content, the researcher might not have been able to tell that they were talking about the same subject.

Recognizing that this is a somewhat distressing thought for researchers, the psychic went on to say in a further reading that, since scientific method is so respected, and indeed almost worshipped today by many who feel that nothing is reliable without it, it is certainly possible to devise researches which prove scientifically whatever is desired—by putting sufficient thought and concentration into the desired results. This, naturally, may not be such a comforting thought to researchers either. The pragmatist comes off somewhat easier in this situation with a belief that "if it works, use it."

Undoubtedly the Dream Helper Project and experiments like it are a powerful tool for group interaction and for the healing which can result.

Chapter Eight

Group Dreaming

Is it possible then to dream in groups? And if so, what does it imply? What are the benefits of group dreaming?

Back in 1954 a psychoanalyst by the name of Kilton Stewart, Ph.D., published an article in *Mental Hygiene* which so excited the dream studying community that it has been mentioned in almost every book about dreams published since that time. The article, "Mental Hygiene and World Peace," compared two Malaysian tribes, the Negrito pygmies of the foothills of the Central Range of mountains of the Malay Peninsula and the Senoi who live in the highlands of that same range.

Although the validity of his observations is now being brought into question by Dr. Richard Benjamin of Cambridge University and explorer Peter Bloch who report no such widespread interest in dreams in the same tribe today, Stewart discusses in the article the differing attitudes toward dreaming of the two "primitive" groups and points out how the Senoi have evolved a "method of education" which "enables his elders to use these (dream) images as channels that assist the child to become a physically healthy, socially constructive, self-possessed adult."

Further, Stewart contends that if modern society were to employ methods similar to the Senoi in the education of its children, that this would promote mental hygiene throughout the world.

What is the Senoi method he discusses? It is quite simply that the members of this primitive culture pay attention to their dreams and the dreams of their children. Over the morning meal, the Senoi discuss the dream events of the night before. Children are encouraged to tell their dreams and discuss the meanings of these dreams. They are encouraged to use the dream material.

In fact, the entire tribe utilizes dreaming in the decision-making process. Over and above listening to the dreams of their children, adult Senoi are guided in their daily work and decisions by their dreams.

Children are taught that if they show hostility or aggression toward someone in a dream, they should apologize and attempt to rectify the attitude in waking life. Similarly, if someone is hostile toward them in a dream, this should be mentioned and some attempt made to understand the cause and generate the cure of the hostility. And, probably most important, Senoi children are taught to develop their personal power of self-confidence through dreams. If they discover a talent or ability in the dream state such as singing or painting, they are not only allowed but encouraged to develop it in the waking state. They are encouraged to face their fears in dreams and send the dreams scampering as parts of the dream reality over which the dreamer has power.

It is this attitude Stewart contends which makes the Senoi a mentally healthy cultural group.

This same emphasis on the importance of dreaming has been pointed out in studies made of the American Indian. And though I personally doubt that we can ever have more than a fairly distorted view of what tribal life was like among our American forebearers, given the fact that tribal belief systems differed so radically from the white culture upon which they were forced to superimpose, and the fact that all Indian tribes have been notoriously reticent about what they consider to be secret and powerful information. still it is possible to assume some basic facts.

One of these is that American Indians as a group placed a fair amount of importance on dreams and a value similar to that of the Senoi. The puberty rites of many Indian groups, particularly the Plains Indians and the Indians of the Southwest, included vision quests or other rituals which required that the adolescent passing the initiation into tribal adulthood be isolated from the tribe for a period of several days.

During this time of separation from the tribe, the youth was expected to fast, to "meditate," and to pay particular attention to any signs including visions or dreams. This was the way in which the youth was given his real name or mystical name, with a full belief that what occurred in the dream or visionary state was as real and more powerful than the events of daily waking life.

The Shamin, or medicine man, was a respected member of Indian society (in those groups which maintain tradition, he still is), and some of the Indians more famous to our history books such as Crazy Horse and Black Elk were in fact powerful tribal leaders because they were led by their dreams and visions.

I have no doubt that were one to carefully scan the entirety of tribal custom, both today and from an historical perspective, that one would find that the bulk of so-called primitive peoples believed more thoroughly in and placed more emphasis on dreams than we do.

Yet, certainly the practical question of any contemporary reader would have to be what does that have to do with modern life? Are there any groups of people living today who place any emphasis on dreams, and what is the result?

Probably the most basic group inside today's societal structure is the family unit and many times, both in and out of dream workshops and seminars, I have heard the comment, "My husband/wife and I always are having the same dream. What does that mean?" You may have heard that comment too, or experienced it yourself.

Apparently many couples have the ability to dream simultaneously, to participate in each other's dreams or even reprogram each other's dreams during the dream state. I have never seen any statistics on the frequency of this phenomenon, nor have I read any studies about it; generally it is passed off as an oddity and something to laugh about.

But I wonder if people who have this ability realize what a unique and potentially therapeutic situation they have? I advise couples who come to me with statements about such occurrences to practice with their dream state and give it some credence. The prospect for enjoyment and adventure as well as for self-understanding are virtually tremendous, and this does not yet mention what could happen if the rest of the family is encouraged to join in the fun.

This sort of dreaming is a corollary to the dream which my writing class student put to me of, "What does it mean if you and your friend both dream you're in the same place at the same time and you both remember it?"

Yet this sort of speculation does not yet begin to answer the question of what can happen if people begin to dream together in groups. My speculation is that, of the many couples and perhaps families who share the ability to dream the same dreams at the same time, almost none of them do anything about it.

In my opinion, one of the essential factors of dream work of any kind is giving the dream some credence, paying some attention to it, utilizing it as something of value.

The Dream Helper Project reported in the last chapter is a single example of how this sort of thing can work. If the event of dreaming with a focus in mind brings people closer together, the event of discussing and pursuing dream meanings is even more intense.

What we are speaking of here, of course, is a willingness not only to enter into the dream state, but an openness to self-examination and communication which terrifies the faint of heart and sometimes frustrates even the strongest. We are speaking of an explora tion of unchartered territories and one which is probably rightly dubbed in Kathleen Jenks' *Journey of A Dream Animal* as the Beyond-Within.

This, I believe, is what holds most people back from dream exploration, the ingrained ingraitating fear that exploration will reveal the nastiest, the deepest and darkest, most hidden and explosive parts of our personalities.

It might, but as I view it after several years of exploration, chances are it won't. Despite all our years of Freudian programming, most of us turn out to be pretty all right guys both on the surface and down toward the core.

What might be discovered, however, is conflict—a conflict of beliefs about what is right and wrong, good and bad; and for the person who is afraid of exploring conflict, any idea of working with dreams should be chucked immediately—let alone the idea of exploring dreams with another person or persons.

Yet, let us go further. For the individual who does want to explore group dreaming, the A.R.E. puts out an enchanting little magazine called the *Sundance Community Dream Journal* which explores many facets of dreaming, a unique magazine in the field.

The true explorers, however, in the field of modern group dreaming are in my opinion the group which focuses around Jane Roberts and her friend Seth. The amount of pioneering work being done here is commendable.

Basically there are two groups about which Jane Roberts writes in her second "Adventures in Consciousness" book, *Psychic Politics*, published in 1976. The first is a group of women to whom the author teaches a writing class; the second is a class which at the time the book was being written was meeting regularly to discuss philosophy and life with Seth, one of the "entities" who "speaks" through Jane Roberts.

In a chapter of *Psychic Politics* entitled "A Probable Class," Jane Roberts discusses some experiments in group dreaming which probably outdistanced any modern experimentation at the time, and may still do so. Not to diminish your pleasure at reading the book itself, let me briefly outline the events discussed in that chapter.

The "probable class" discussed in that chapter is, in fact, the culmination of a series of experiments with altered states of consciousness which has been informally conducted by Jane Roberts Butts and Rob Butts and their friends for some time, beginning with the publication of Jane's first Seth book in 1963. By the time recorded in this chapter some members of the group had been together and experimenting for five and more years, thus fulfilling the first priority for effective group dreaming which is giving some credence to the dream state.

In the chapter under discussion, members of Jane's regular Monday night Seth class share a "dream class" or class in another probable reality system which several of them recall, with varying degrees of similarity in the recall experience. For Jane herself the dream event was a lucid dream in which she was aware she was dreaming and told other members of the group that this was a "probable class." For other members of the group, the "class" had been more of an ordinary dream event, but one thing stands out. Each time that either of the classes meets, group members discuss the previous week's dreams and experiences. They give credence to these events.

One student, Mary, recalled no dream events the night of Jane's lucid dream, but had been re-reading a chapter in one of the Seth books which described her only to-that-time recalled out of body experience. She had fallen asleep at almost precisely the time Jane recalled the dream event happening and had appeared in the hallway in Jane's dream calling out that she was there.

Another student, Ben, described his experience at that time as a "half-awake, half-asleep state" in which he was attending an ESP class where they were discussing the regular class of that same evening. Events in his dream correlated with events in Jane's dream.

Other students also reported their similar experiences, some of which centered around Rob and a farm or farmhouse which had been described by one student as seeing Rob in a plowing contest.

Obviously the events reported here are inconclusive, much as the events reported in the earlier discussion of the Dream Helper Project were inconclusive, and Jane Roberts summarizes her chapter with the observation that once people begin to observe their experiences with altered states of consciousness or "other realities" they can be not only time consuming but disconcerting and that for the experienced dreamer, the simple act of recording the night's dream events can take up to an hour a day.

This is something which I have noticed myself and which is certainly a complaint heard from others who begin to seriously study their dreams, but the question still remains of what use can this group attention to dreaming be?

I would like to record here a history of some experimentation done with group dreaming at Poseidia Institute, and my own answers to the above question. Surely we will never really know the usefulness of group dreaming or dreaming of any kind until we give it a chance to work, any more than we could know the usefulness of, say, the Salk polio vaccine until experiments were conducted.

Some six years ago, when Poseidia Institute came into existence as the Association for Documentation and Enlightenment (the name was later changed to avoid confusion with the A.R.E.), one of the first classes offered was a dream workshop. As a participant in that workshop I readily noticed that there was a higher than average incidence of lucid dreaming among the group members—everyone having had at least one lucid dreaming experience and many having had regular lucid dreams. I filed this bit of information away, putting it down to the fact that this group was more than casually interested in dreams.

However, out of my own interest in dreams I kept a mental note of how often the members of the organization, particularly those with developed psychic talents, talked about dreams which were lucid or precognitive or out of the ordinary in some other way and again noticed what seemed to be an unusually high incidence of such events.

At the time the organization had no paid staff and was run on a strictly voluntary basis, its goals being the development of new approaches to health, and illness prevention.

When I became director of the organization's growing paid and volunteer staff in the Fall of 1976, a dream event tipped me off to the importance of keeping a focus on dreams within the group and we began to discuss dreams at weekly staff meetings and in other meetings around the office. The dream event which triggered this interest was as follows.

On the morning of November 29th, I mentioned to Ellen Andrews-Negus, then the organization's only working psychic, that she had been in my dream the night before. She laughed and said I had also been in her dream of the previous night and the dream had been really unusual. Her dream was:

> I am giving readings outside and in front of a crowd. I do a reading for a dark-haired girl named Meg and the crowd is impressed. I start another reading but am interrupted by an airplane and the arrival of Janice. As I am talking to Janice I slip back into trance and tell her, "Your addictive problems with your parents are just about over." Jean Campbell is there smiling at me. Jean and I are sitting on the ground looking at the

sky. I tell her I'm not happy with my readings. She disappears. The sky turns into a large glass box that is tied up with a brown ribbon that has a white section running down the middle. The ribbon ties itself into a bow and I say, "This means I have everything too neatly packaged."

Later that same day Ellen did a reading at her home which in part said the following:

Good evening, Ellen and Jean. This is a reading for both of you. Ellen has been requesting information concerning her own creativity and the readings and Jean has been asking some of these same questions, although less consciously. The answers to these were given to you mutually last night in the dream state but Ellen did not really understand the symbology of that wrapped package—which will be untied slowly throughout 1977.

The reading goes on to outline some of the events which will be taking place in the coming year, concluding with:

The most important idea we wish to get across now is that you need psychics of the type who can easily accommodate individual readings. When the phenomenon is better understood (yes, we'll do some sessions on the subject), research oriented psychics will not expend creative energy in fields which they are not "wired" for. For Ellen, the proofs of the validity of the phenomenon have become well established. Now her attention can be gradually turned to the next step.

Coordination points are not simply geographically located areas of incoming energy. Coordination points exist within the spectrum of consciousness and are symbolized outwardly not only by places but by people; the prophets, leaders of government, geniuses, artists, musicians, etc. The energy of the coordination point is translated by factors inherent within the personality involved and appear outwardly in various ways. Psychics are one type of coordination point. In terms of Ellen, there is one type of ability that dominates, and other psychics will be provided that cover other areas of the spectrum.

Keep up the classes. The energy of ADE (Poseidia) itself is designed to pass along the ability to view the spectrum of consciousness in new and different ways.

Before going on, a few explanations are in order. The trance psychics who work for Poseidia Institute doing a wide variety of readings, though they do not channel a particular entity such as Seth, describe experiences of the trance phenomenon very similar to those described by Jane Roberts in her books and by Edgar Cayce in his mongraph from a lecture on what a reading is.

The subject of coordination points, mentioned in the above reading was a subject of interest to me at the time, described by Seth in the volume *Seth Speaks*. Ellen had not read any of the Jane Roberts material at that time nor, to my knowledge, was she consciously familiar with the subject of coordination points.

It is an interesting aside to note that an individual who had not yet developed her trance ability, Christi Anna Davidson, a trance psychic who later worked part-time for Poseidia Institute, recorded a dream which took place at approximately the same time as the dream Ellen and I shared. In that dream Christi Anna said:

I am supposed to go in a helicopter. I'm hesitant. Since I have to go, I decide I'd rather go in the large helicopter and sit in the midst of the group where I will not have to see out the window. However, I'm maneuvered into a two-person helicopter with Ellen Andrews-Negus. There is no visible pilot unless we ask questions. Then he appears, answers the questions and becomes invisible again.

This is the first in a series of dreams recorded by Christi Anna as she developed her psychic ability in which going up in an airplane symbolized the trance state of consciousness. The pilot is generally invisible; Ellen is frequently present; and as her talents develop the plane gradually changes from a helicopter to an ordinary airplane to a jet.

In Ellen's dream of November 28th she is interrupted in giving a reading by the sound of an airplane.

The record of this event certainly prodded me into a greater awareness of dreaming within the group and eventually the interest has grown as more "unusual" events have taken place. These events are not limited to staff members, or to psychics, but take place throughout the group of people connected with Poseidia. I will record here a few of them. You will notice that their frequency increases as we move toward the present.

In the early days of the organization I had more than once dreamed about the group in terms of making music together and was not at all surprised when one of Ellen's readings made the analogy that directorship of this group was like conducting a symphony orchestra with the group members being the instruments. I personally enjoy music a great deal and many of my dreams involve music. One of my first recorded dreams about the group back in 1974 was:

> I was in a room in what appeared to be a medieval castle or court. The window openings were set high in the wall and sunlight was streaming through them. The walls were lined with instruments of various kinds. Several people came in and I handed them instruments. Ted came in. I handed him a lute. He said he didn't know how to play it but I said I could teach him to play.

This was one of the dreams which, as I mentioned earlier, I had learned to detect as more than strictly personal. There was very much the feeling of the group being involved here. The music dreams, as I call them, had however been strictly my own until in August of 1978 the head of Poseidia's Counseling Center, psychologist Lore Aloro, told me one morning that she had awakened that morning from a dream where she had been composing a very beautiful modern melody. She woke with the music still in her mind, but being unable to write musical notation in waking reality, she had allowed the music to slip away.

I was amused to hear her dream because that same morning I had recorded the following:

> I was looking at a painting of a piano and wondered what it would look like from another angle. Then I found myself looking at the same painting with a third dimension added. A pianist was seated at the piano and I heard him playing Moussorgsky's *Pictures at an Exhibition.*
>
> Then I found myself in a hall looking at the same pianist; an orchestra was seated nearby and had picked up the tune. I looked behind me and I was in a large auditorium with tiers of bleachers. Poseidia members were seated in the bleachers and many of them sang and hummed along. I went to a corner where Ellen was explaining to someone how to do readings.

If I had needed any convincing that Lore was "tuned in," an event which happened shortly before this had convinced me completely. She came into the office one morning saying with a laugh that she dreamed the night before that Ellen had been giving her a reading. When she looked in her mailbox at almost the same time she was telling me this, she paled. In her box was a reading which Ellen, having prepared to give a reading the night before for one of the many individuals who request readings from Poseidia, had instead given for Lore. Ellen had not known until she awoke from

trance that the reading had been for Lore. Lore had no foreknowledge that the reading would take place.

The second of Lore's musical dreams came in October when
she dreamed:

> I find myself in a bare room except for a piano and
> an open cot on which Rodney (another counselor) is
> lying or half reposing with his head in his hand. I am
> seated at the piano playing a beautiful contemporary
> piano concerto—it was very unusual in that it was
> melodious. I played beautifully. I thought that odd since
> I have never learned how to play except for a few notes. I
> actually hear the music in the dream and I get very
> excited watching my hands fly over the keyboard. I'm
> fascinated and amazed because I'm so forceful and sure
> of myself. I laugh and think "Horowitz would like this
> interpretation."
>
> As I end what appears to be a movement, I turn
> around and see Rodney with a cigarette. He says, "Just
> one; that's all I can allow myself." (This statement can
> only be understood when realizing that we had dis-
> cussed our "last addiction," the addiction to fear, the
> night before.)
>
> I continue to play, but this time I find the keyboard
> covered with books. This doesn't seem to phase me—I
> simply move the books to have access to the keys and
> finish the piece with a flourish. At this point I get up,
> go to the window, open it and say, "Nino won't like the
> smell of smoke. We must let the fresh air in." Then I
> wake up.

Lore adds, "This dream was one that came during the night
when I asked for some sign of whether or not I truly could develop
my intuitive abilities in order to be the kind of counselor who
could successfully work with the kinds of clients I was getting.
These are mostly on the brink of developing their intuitive or
psychic potential."

The dreams by no means have concerned just the central core
of staff at Poseidia. A few examples of some of the dreams which
have been reported to me include people living in areas distant
from one another, and sometimes unknown to one another.

One member, a woman who had been plagued since her
childhood with precognitive dreams presaging the death of friends
or members of the family and who, like others, was helped through
Poseidia to understand that she was not causing the deaths or
accidents but only perceiving them, said that she knew in 1977
from a dream that she would be learning astrology from someone

with a strong Sagittarian influence who loved purple and that person would be an important teacher to her. The dream took the form of a vision in which she was projected out into the galaxy to stand within the circle of the zodiac, each sign being represented by its glyph. The Sagittarian centaur had stepped forward ringed in purple. Despite the attempts of friends to persuade her to take astrology from another Sagittarian teacher, our dreamer refused and held out for the right one.

In January of 1978, astrologer Mike Shoemaker joined the staff of Poseidia having recently retired from the U.S. Air Force. One day while he was sitting in the office, the member whose dream predicted such a teacher saw him and immediately asked the secretary if Mike was an astrology teacher, and did he like purple. Startled, Mike answered that purple was his favorite color. His moon is located in the sign of Sagittarius.

An equally dramatic report came from another female member who was taking an art course through Poseidia. She also took private lessons from the instructor, Robert Willis, who was planning to move to Texas shortly after the conclusion of the course. The two became very close and Willis had expressed a desire to see Pat, the dreamer, learn as much as she could from him before he left so she could teach the techniques to others.

Pat said that she had dreamed occasionally of being in drawing class, but one day she came to the office brimming over with excitement. The night before she had gone to bed with a particular problem in mind, not knowing how to solve it. That same night she had an art lesson in which she was given step by step instruction on how to solve the problem.

Delighted, the next morning she called Willis and told him she had dreamed about him, then outlined the dream lesson. Not only had she received exactly the correct solution to her dream problem in just the way her instructor would have given it to her in waking life, but he admitted at that point that he often dreamed he was giving lessons to particular students.

As a whole the group at Poseidia found that the more attention they paid to dreams, the more attention the dreams paid to them.

In 1977 when the decision was pending to move the organization from the building which was then its headquarters, there developed a spate of dreams about the "new building." Though in fact we moved into a suite of offices in a professional building, whatever spark of imagination fired the dream, it must have been the same spark because I heard from no less than half a dozen people about the large white stucco building with fireplaces and wrought iron gates which we would purchase. I spoke with these people independently of one another. They, for the most part, did not know about each other well at all. Yet they all described driving or walking up to the same white stucco walls, the same wide veranda and seeing large, spacious rooms inside. I am still not convinced that this is "just a dream," but it certainly is a mass phenomenon which has not yet manifested in waking reality.

I often conduct office business during the dream state and am quite aware of doing it, as sometimes are the people who share the dream. The dream state is particularly good for solving conflicts and smoothing over ruffled feathers because in the dream state we tend to have far less of a barrier and are more honest about our emotions than in the waking state.

I wrote earlier about dealing with student difficulties in this manner and find it works just as well in the office situation. Often I will think about a particular person or problem before I fall asleep, and ask for dream guidance. Sometimes the person just shows up.

I was required to let one staff member go, for example, an unpleasant situation under any circumstances. Though I realized the need for the act, I was distressed at the antagonism it generated and had a series of dreams. In one dream before the person was fired I found myself arguing in the dream state with her saying, "If you don't do thus and so, I'm going to have to fire you," trying to convince her to change her ways.

She continued to appear in my dreams for several weeks after she was fired, sometimes arguing, sometimes listening, until finally one evening I said to her, "You feel pretty good about the matter now, don't you?" She noded her assent and I went on with my dream.

How do I know these dream characters are not just symbolic, that they actually are there and I'm communicating with them? As I've said before it's a sense I've developed and which other people seem to have developed also, an inner knowing which figure is more "real" than "symbol." Remember what I've said about the nature of reality and the symbolic nature of waking life and you'll see the amusing side of this statement. But there is a developable sense of how close the dream is to waking reality.

In addition to this, this type of awareness is something we practice and teach in classes at Poseidia. A class assignment in psychic development and other classes is for class members to choose a time and location at which they will meet during the dream state to pursue a particular activity. Generally this works quite nicely for at least some of the group.

An example of this type of class activity is a class that I took one day for a session near the ocean. After class four of the class members spontaneously decided to get together that night in the same spot. Because they had been working with their dreams for a while, they had results even under adverse conditions. One group member entered the lucid state and clearly remembered floating down to see three figures seated on the selected hilltop, then his telephone rang. One member got no sleep that night because her little girl was sick. One member remembered no dreams. And the fourth member remembered being in a group of people around a fire on a sand dune.

Of course this session by itself is totally inconclusive, as are any of the incidents related here; but taken as a group, they become more interesting.

I spoke earlier of the dream where I asked Ellen Andrews-Negus the next day if she remembered the dream we had. She did—i.e., we both remembered being in the dream and being aware of each other being in the dream. The frequency of this type of dream is not so great as some other types of events which I'll record here.

One day a few days after the above situation occurred, I again asked Ellen if she remembered the dream we had. She said she didn't remember any dreams for that night, but asked for mine. I had dreamed that I was on a train. Ellen was there already seated when I got on. I looked out the window and saw beautiful mountains. I said to Ellen, "Let's go together. Where are you going?" She said she was going to Denver. I had a moment of regret because I'd planned to go to Philadelphia.

When I told her the dream, Ellen laughed because before going to sleep the night before she had been looking through her new copy of *National Geographic*. The thing which had held her interest was a beautiful color spread on Denver. On the other hand, though in the dream I traveled along with her, Philadelphia is my symbol for freedom (liberty) and I frequently travel there.

Another incident of the same sort happened when one of the members of the Board of Trustees telephoned from Tuscon, Arizona, where she had moved from Virginia Beach some months before. Due to the long distance rates, she had never telephoned and is not a letter writer. On the morning of her phone call she told me, " I was dreaming about you last night and it was so clear that I wondered if you'd been thinking about me,"

Sadly, I had not; but I *had* been reading Anya Seaton's novel *Foxfire* which is set in Arizona; and, before going to bed the previous night, had been very moved by her beautiful descriptions of Indian life in the Tucson area. This dream might be put in the context of the phone call game, which I came to notice because of its greater-than-chance occurrence in my office. My manner of organization is that each morning, or sometimes the night before, I make a list of things I have to accomplish during the day and people I have to contact. I soon discovered that, working with a group of people who at least to some degree allow their intuitive abilities to become part of their daily lives, I was not having to make the telephone calls because the people themselves would either call or come into the office—a very efficient system as far as I am concerned.

A final dream incident I found to be more interesting and less amusing. One of the very active members of the organization is a retired orthopedic surgeon with whom I traveled one weekend to attend a meeting in Washington, D.C.

One evening the doctor did not appear when and where he was expected. But I and others thought he had probably gotten lost in the maze of Washington area roads; and, since there was no way to contact him, had returned to our rooms assuming we would hear from him. That evening I had the following dream:

> I met George (the doctor) in a greeting card shop. He was showing me cards, contemporary cards. The first one said "KARMA" on the cover. The message inside read, "It's all over." The second card bore the words "GROW UP" on the cover. Inside it read, "You've got to do it sometime." The third card, which I did not have time to read, had a black star of David on the cover. It was a sympathy card.

I learned the next day that my friend had suffered a massive cardiac arrest on his way to meet us and, discovered by a passing motorist, had been taken to the intensive care unit of a local hospital.

Let's return for a moment to the question of the implications of group dreaming and its possible uses. In my opinion, the few incidents cited in this chapter give rise to some interesting speculations which lead us to some even more interesting conclusions.

First I think we must recognize that those who talk of there being no more frontiers are ignoring the final, and perhaps the most exciting frontier, that of the mind.

If the implications of this chapter are correct even in part, the possibilites for self-understanding and for communication are virtually limitless even though it may be necessary to accept a time and space frame different from the one we currently accept as real.

If what is discussed here is true then, through the medium of dreams or dream-like states, it should be possible to develop the ability to travel, to visit friends in another part of the country or the world with as much recognition and recall as in the waking state. It should be possible to decide upon a location or time to explore and to do so.

The possibilities for communication are limitless, the casual conversation, the solution of problems which are difficult even to approach in the waking state, the carrying on of business details, and so on.

Once again we return to the question of credibility. Are these possibilites real or imaginary? Discounting events which we hear have happened with the sages of India, "primitive" or "uncivilized" tribal cultures, or American Indian mystics such as Carlos Castaneda's Don Juan, I must say that the first step toward exploring the dazzling possibilities of the dream world is to approach it with an open mind as well as one which is rational and questioning. The dream events discussed here are real and have taken place in the recent past among ordinary people. They are, I am sure, not as far as it is possible to go with dreams; but nevertheless they are a step. And, in certainty, the more attention the dream state is given, the more flexible the dream world becomes.

Chapter Nine

A Week's Worth Of Dreams

The final two chapters of this book are devoted to the learning of how to better deal with dreams, dream exercises, and dream interpretations.

Because it is often difficult to see what to do with dreams without viewing someone else's consistent, ongoing dreams, I have chosen at random a week's worth of my own dreams and will annotate the process through which I traveled to gain understanding of them. The process itself, by this stage in my own dream development is sometimes much abbreviated from what I have given here; and I think any dreamer must be careful of two things: 1) not to get so involved with the dream world as to think every dream is of the utmost importance as a message or lesson, or sometimes even an accurate perception of "reality;" and 2) not to allow dream studies to take such an inordinate amount of time that they take away the balance of other everyday activities. I sometimes go for long periods of time at this point without writing down or even paying much attention to the dream world, but that comes from an awareness of inner feelings that tells me when paying attention to dreams will be most helpful in working out problems or understanding a situation.

The following dreams come from the week preceding a time when I would be called upon to play hostess to a fairly large membership conference and, additionally, I knew that my former husband would be attending the conference. It was a fairly highly-charged emotional period and I used my dreams to help sort out and analyze my feelings prior to the conference. There are, you'll notice, also some interesting dreams of other types during the week.

> Friday, August 4, 1978—I am with Margie and we are talking about our planned trip to France, but Margie keeps dallying around and I finally get bored and leave.

For me this dream needs no interpretation since the symbols are all familiar, but in a way I am giving myself a statement about the coming week much like previews at a movie theatre.

Margie and I were both members of a group of people who, after we finished graduate school together, decided we would like to live in intentional community. The community failed, as many do, because the group could not meet the emotional demands of close, daily encounter. My life at the time of the dream was also as part of a community, but a much less focalized and physically close one. In this instance, since Margie and I had recently re-established contact after several years of not writing to one another, she represented not only the prior community, but that group of my former friends who were now comfortable with my current lifestyle.

France also is a frequent dream symbol for me, much as in my dreams Philadelphia represents freedom or brotherly love. France is a symbol for closeness, hospitality, familiarity and old attitudes.

I have never traveled in France, yet French was the only foreign language I ever chose to study. I sometimes speak French in my dreams, though in waking life my command of the language is only moderate. I have been told by more than one psychic of life experiences in France, particularly one in the 13th century where I was a nun in a cloistered order, another type of voluntary community.

Margie, the friend in the dream, although she is a Quaker, has been compared by more than one friend to a nun; and I once had a party experience in this lifetime where I, being only slightly stoned, suddenly saw several members of the company in rough brown habits.

All of this is both relevant and irrelevant to the dream message which was making a comparision between my former "community" and my present "community," stating that they were not yet the same. Yet the dream is a very clear example of the working of dream symbology where layer upon layer of personal symbology can be translated into a few pictures. Whether or not experiences in other "lifetimes" play any part in this dream or this lifetime is irrelevant except that these experiences have obvious emotional connotations for me—emotional connotations which I was at the time of the dream trying to work through.

Saturday, August 5, 1978—Lucid dream. I awoke and put my hand through the sheet. I was aware that I was dreaming. Put my feet over the side of the bed and drifted over to the dresser, then out the bedroom door and into the living room where Sam (not his real name) was lying on the couch. He was awake.

We talked about the changes he would have to make. At the end of the conversation I said to him, "It's going to be hard, do you think you can make it?" He said yes, he thought he could. I awoke in present reality in my own bed.

We had a weekend visitor that weekend, a young man who is a member of Poseidia and who was experiencing a great deal of emotional turmoil in his life. We had spent the day in some fairly intense conversation. But he was not extremely easy to communicate with because of his natural barriers, and so I was taking this evening opportunity to talk with him.

I asked him the next day if he remembered our dream conversation. He said no. How do I know that I wasn't imagining it, that the dream didn't have some message in it meant for me?

Well, first of all, there is a different feeling associated with a lucid dream, much more of an ordinary-waking-reality feeling. I "awoke," knew I was dreaming, and decided to visit Sam because he'd been having trouble and was much more open to communication—all while in the dream state.

This does not eliminate either the so-called imaginary element, or the symbolic element if it is true that we create or participate in the creation of our waking reality as well as our dream reality. Sam was just as much of a symbol while I was awake as when I was asleep; and, in fact, did in some way symbolize the struggle I was then going through to integrate certain portions of myself. He was highly intuitive, highly sensitive, and struggling to trust the people in his environment enough to aid himself. If we are willing to take it as such, my question to him of, "Do you think you can make it?" can be taken as another aspect of the statement made by Christi Anna in the dream helper reading: "There is no 'your problem,' or 'our problem,' or 'their problem.' No 'my growth,' or 'your growth' or 'our growth' or 'their growth.' It is a oneness." This is a difficult, but helpful concept; and certainly takes one away from the savior concept or the belief that anyone needs to be saved from anything.

Sunday, August 6, 1978—I dreamed that I came out of the front door at my mother's house. John (my former husband) was in the side yard with a large hoop in his hand. He was encouraging a green and blue parrot or love bird to fly through the hoop, and it was doing so with the air of one who is not quite convinced.

John was saying to me, "Look. See what I can get it to do!" Then the parrot flew to a perch on the side porch. I noticed that there was another parrot, probably its mate, who was flying alone high in the air, doing lazy circles and spins with great grace. The other parrot glided in for a landing beside the first one.

I awoke from this dream totally mystified as to its meaning. I had never before dreamed anything like it or even remotely resembling it. So I decided to gestalt the dream and let the dream characters speak for themselves. Generally when I gestalt a dream, the first character or object I ask to speak is the one which carries the greatest emotional impact. In this case it was immediately clear. The lovebird who was flying through the hoop began speaking almost without request.

She, and there was no doubt from that moment that she was a *she*, said, "Look what he *thinks* he can make me do. I fly through that hoop only to please him, only to be nice to him." She looked over her shoulder at her mate who was doing high-flying swoops and glides in the air.

The message of the dream became immediately clear to me when I compared the two birds, especially when I recognized that the name of her mate was Leonard—also the name of my present mate. This little lovebird was only pretending not to be free, and her action was much as mine had been in pretending to jump through hoops for John while all the time knowing it was just a game.

It is interesting to note that I chose the lovebirds as a symbol, not only because I frequently dream about birds (in this case quite a domesticated bird), but because one of my former students, who reminds me a great deal of Leonard, keeps a lovebird as a pet and his lovebird is given great freedom to fly around the house. There is the feeling of security that I get from these two people, knowing that it is acceptable to fly, to test one's wings.

The action of the dream took place at "my mother's house," again, where my dreams frequently occur. And in this case I readily called it my mother's house, not my childhood home as I sometimes do. My mother, like the female lovebird, taught me to be concerned about what other people thought, about pleasing people. In the dream, as I sometimes do in waking life, I very neatly represented the female side of myself as aquiescent to jumping through hoops, while the male side of myself—the agressive, creative part of me—flew high in the sky and only swooped down to be with me.

I had a little conversation with the male lovebird.

"Do you ever get lonely up there?"

"Not as long as I have you to come back to."

"Do you ever feel tied down?"

"Sometimes I wish we could just fly away together, and be free."

Monday, August 7, 1978, nap—I was riding a motorcycle on a super highway that had a lot of high-speed entrance and exit ramps. The day was sunny and clear. I was cruising along at a high speed, when suddenly I discovered a UFO, a large, round, flying saucer in the middle of the road. There were people cordoning the area and aliens were getting out of the flying saucer. I felt like they might get me.

I turned the bike and raced down an exit ramp where I found myself almost immediately on a dirt road and riding into a carnival or small country fair. It was twilight. The lights were on on the merry-go-round. I stopped the bike and got off.

Again this dream contained symbols already familiar to me, and some that were not. In order to understand the full import of the dream, I looked at the colors, the feelings, the sounds portrayed here.

In this dream, it begins to become clear that what I am dealing with is more than a simple concern over what will happen in the weekend upcoming. At a dream level, especially during this week when my waking hours are filled with preparations for the conference, my dream self is dealing with underlying conflicts represented by disparate aspects of myself.

I begin this dream scene roaring down a superhighway in broad daylight on a motorbike. In waking life all this time I was learning to drive an automobile, a skill which I had never previously learned—always being too involved with other things to want to become involved with such an "aggressive, mechanical thing." In waking life I had never learned to drive a motorcycle, considering this ever more dangerous than driving a car, with more risk of accident and danger to life and limb. As an aside, my mother did not drive a car when I was growing up, nor did my only sister learn to drive until she was in her mid-thirties. I suspect that there was a strong part of me that was simply convinced that driving was not a proper feminine thing to do. Yet here I was in waking life, learning to drive; and here I was in dream life, racing along on a motorbike.

Everything was fine until I suddenly confronted a UFO—an unidentified, spooky, unknown.

"Who are you?" I asked one of the aliens.

"We're visiting from another planet. Everyone knows we're ok. Look at this crowd around our ship. They're not carrying guns. They're just curious."

"Don't you ever hurt anyone?"

"Not unless we're attacked first and have to defend ourselves."

"Don't you ever mistake a friendly overture for an attack?"

"Occasionally, but it really is easy to tell who's being friendly. Most people are, you know. You are too even though sometimes you think you're being too aggressive."

Not having the benefit of this conversation in the dream, however; and being afraid of attack from this unknown force, I retreated to the dirt road, to the twilight, to the rustic carnival atmosphere that to me so clearly represents security.

Monday, August 7, 1978, night—I am with John and Ed and we are going to a restaurant, a fancy restaurant and we are all dressed up. John goes on ahead. The restaurant is below street level, beneath a theatre. I find myself alone in a cafeteria-like kitchen which is very smoky or hazy. A lone girl, looking somewhat starving and bedraggled is sitting at a long table eating meatballs. A heavy man in a greasy teeshirt and a tall white chef's cap lounges against the wall watching her eat.

The conflict at this point had clearly become more than a conflict set up by seeing an old relationship in new company. John, who had been appearing in my dreams on an almost daily basis, went on ahead, went out of the picture—and, for that matter, has not appeared since. I was left alone in the kitchen with the "cook" and a starving, bedraggled female.

The location of the restaurant is in itself a clue. It is underground, subliminal, below street level—and located beneath a theatre which Shakespeare so aptly typified when he claimed, "All the world's a stage."

Beneath the stage of my waking life lived this smoky kitchen. I spoke first to the cook.

"Who are you?"

"I'm the cook."

"Obviously, you're the cook, but what are you doing here?" (I was annoyed by the slow, comfortable manner of this man who lounged against the wall, his arms folded across his big belly.)

"I fix food." (His eyes were twinkling. I felt like he was laughing at me. I turned to the girl who was busy spooning food into her face, apparently unaware of my presence.)

For a long time I had been aware that food, like all the dream books tell us, was symbolic of sustenance—the staff of life, and if this girl was I, she was evidently starving. She was eating meatballs; and, always sensitive to the clues my dreams give me, I concluded two things: one, if red meat (as this obviously was, and covered with red sauce) represented the male, aggressive nature (as is taught by Buddhists and nutritionists alike), then I obviously was starved for that; and two, if on another level red meat is in moderation, good for the body, then it might be physically beneficial for me to add a little more red meat to my diet. I am not a strict vegetarian or a strict anything else, but do tend to follow a diet which is fairly light in red meat.

I returned my attention to the cook. "You're her friend, aren't you?"

"Sure," he said, "and I'd be yours too if you weren't so afraid of me. There's nothing wrong with a little masculinity, you know."

All of a sudden, while talking to this dream character in my "imagination," I became aware of the sexual nature of his stance and the fact that the down-home, New Orleans jazz patois, of which I am so fond, speaks of the kitchen and sex in one breath. This was that kind of a kitchen.

The female, who came to look more and more like me during this conversation, never looked up. She was simply starving for some of this down-home comfort and looked as if she would murder the first person who tried to take it away from her.

As the conference approached, my real, underlying fears began to surface. In my job as director I had taken on a role which previously I had not confronted. I was a female playing a traditionally male role, and the conference would only make that more public. Part of me, like my mother, said, "A woman's place is in the home. Women are non-aggressive. It is unacceptable to be aggressive, to be creative, to be free or to be flexible." The other part of me obviously did not agree, and took one role after another in my dreams to try to convince me that what I was doing was good and proper. Meanwhile on the daily stage of my life, I went on as if there were no conflict. Getting a little too close to the mark, I skipped a night of dream recall. By this time, it's a pretty sure sign of resistance to me if I don't log at least one dream per day.

Wednesday, August 9, 1978, Dream #1—I am trying on clothes in my room at home. I try on a blue, loose cut, knee-length terry cloth robe and a floor-length, frilly, pink lace evening dress.

Dream #2—I am on stage in a high school auditorium dressed like a flapper, singing *Second Hand Rose*.

Dream #3—I am in the subway, getting onto a subway train. There is dim lighting and more action which I can't remember.

In all these dreams I am both acting and observing myself acting from some distance above and in front of myself. One of the nice things about the dream state is that it is possible with awareness to play two or more roles in the dream and watch yourself doing it as well.

Just like counterpoint, the theme of all three of these dreams revolves around the question of my role and how I see myself in it. For me, perhaps because when I first began working on dreams with a group, we all accepted the interpretation that changing clothes meant changing roles, trying on clothes always designated trying on roles.

In the first dream I am in the bedroom of my childhood home, where I first began to see myself as individual enough to have a role, and I am trying on first a blue, boy-color outfit, the terry-cloth robe. It is loose fitting and comfortable. I feel good in it. Then I try on a pink, girl-color outfit, the pink, lace evening dress. It is scratchy and uncomfortable. Once again I tell myself in the dream state that the male role is one in which I feel comfortable.

You may say that this is a very brief and seemingly incomplete analysis of this dream, as well it may be since I am familiar with my own particular symbols. And I think it deserves repeating here, with these three fragmentary and almost innocuous dreams to repeat that there are many ways of coming to an understanding of dream symbols.

One of the approaches to this dream might have been to take any object, *any* object, and to have done a simple free word association with it. Take the terry-cloth robe for example. When I free associate with this, which in fact I did but very, very quickly, I come up with: comfort, comforting, Harry (the name of someone who gave me a robe similar to this) man, manstyle, blue, boy-color. As you can see, just relaxing I was letting my mind go to feelings and events surrounding this particular object.

The second dream is perhaps even a better example of this type of free association. On the surface of things this dream is one of those where I might laugh and say jokingly to someone the next day, "Boy, did I have a strange dream last night. I dreamed I was dressed up like a flapper doing a Barbra Streisand number."

But let's take a little closer look (not that the dream wasn't funny or that there would be anything wrong with such a comment). I have found as you might have also, that in my waking life, I generally have what I used to call a "radio playing in my head." That is that almost continuously, somewhere just below the level of the general chatter of my thoughts, there is music going on. Sometimes it's a symphony; sometimes it's a television commercial; sometimes it's a particular song with words. Usually, if I concentrate, I can tune in on what particular tune is playing. This phenomenon may occur simply because I enjoy music and am myself musical; but I have talked with others who also have their own music playing.

I used to think that this was just a nice thing that happened in my head, that I had music playing, until one day several years ago I had listened to an argument which was raging between three of my friends. A fourth friend asked me my opinion of the argument and simultaneously I tuned on on what my mental radio was playing. It was "Three Blind Mice."

I decided to experiment and before long determined that whatever was happening in the outer world, I was not only getting music; I was getting musical commentary.

So when I came across *Second Hand Rose* in my dream, I did not just grin and ignore it as I might have sometime ago. Once again I started to listen. The lines that I heard ran:
"Even the piano in the parlor
Papa bought for ten cents on the dollar."
Those lines repeated. I didn't even know the other verses of the song.

When I was a child I was fascinated by a piano which my older married brother and his wife left at our house while they moved. This piano opened up a whole new world for me and I soon learned to pick out tunes on it. For the remainder of my childhood, after they removed that piano, I coveted the pianos my friends owned and were forced to learn to play. Every day I prayed for a piano, but we were poor and the day was a long time in coming. When we finally did get a piano several years later, it too was second hand, and like that of "Second Hand Rose," cost $25 with the sheet music included. That piano and its contents came, rightly or wrongly, to represent to me my family's, especially my father's, attitude toward my creative ability as well as toward my needs and desires. Whereas I considered a piano the most important thing in the world—far beyond pretty clothes, or food—to my father it was a luxury, purchasable only after the important things were bought.

The dream, simple as it seemed, summed up all the bittersweet memories of my childhood, which said, "Don't be too up front (masculine, aggressive, creative) about what you want. You'll only get hurt."

In the third dream, which I conveniently forgot, I was in the subway, for me a familiar dream territory. Like the subterranean restaurant in the previous night's dream, the subway is, for me, the signal for receiving information from the most hidden levels of my being.

Thursday, August 10, 1978—I am walking through a Gauguin forest of tropical lushness, a forest veld. There is a man with me (a shadow). It is about twilight and the forest takes on a milky, pearly hue—dusk, quiet, elevating. Someone says, "This area is being mined now."

We continue to walk, and a few feet in front of us sits a larger-than-life native woman. She also looks like a Gauguin—brown-skinned, large-eyed, sensual with black, coarse hair flowing past her shoulders. She was very large and sat cross-legged like a goddess or idol on the ground of a large clearing filled with very green grass. She did not look up, but continued to count something from a pile on the ground into a basket. The same speaker as before said, "She used to take twenty seeds of this, thirty pieces of that."

Then my shadow companion and I lay down and fell asleep in the clearing. Someone threw a rough, green wool army blanket over us.

At about the same time the blanket was thrown over us, I "awoke" to see a man rushing out the front door of my mother's house shouting, "They've moved the war office!"

In a later part of the dream a blond girl who looked like Susan rode up to my mother's house very fast on a bicycle. She was mad, and steamed in more ways than one.

Almost as if I subconsciously chose to use every trick and device known to dream analysis in this one week of dreaming (not to mention working through a very real problem of my own) this dream comes in the form of a vision giving everything the luminescent quality, the musical brightness of an archetypal vision, complete with a very Jungian shadow.

The scene takes place in a forest (which I sometimes have trouble seeing for the trees), in a clearing. The figure beside me, although more of a *non-figure* than anything else is definitely male and very definitely of the variety that Jung labels "the shadow," that numinous form which lives within each of us. The first words spoken by the off-scene narrator, that sort of *deus ex machina* who enters many people's dreams, are, *"This area is being mined now."*

The statement clearly means that this is something I've gotten down to, as the miner digs for ore; but the hyperbole is also clear in that "this area is being made mine now." All of these things are devices which many dreamers use. You might also be surprised, if you were to analyze as carefully a few hours' thought patterns—including the fleeting words and pictures which cross the mind—to find, as I have, that any moment's thoughts are as carefully laced with layer upon layer of symbol, each one triggering a particular thought or emotional response. One of the reasons I qualify this particular episode as a vision or vision-like is because of the emotional tone pattern which it sets off, that of a deep, awe-inspiring chord or melody, which says, "This is right."

In the dream my shadow and I next encounter a "Gauguin-type female," of the kind so frequently depicted by that artist during his stay in the South Sea Islands. She is dark, long-haired (as I am myself), and larger-than-life size. She sits placidly, quite ignoring our presence, counting objects into a basket. She is self-contained, relaxed, and confident. The unseen voice says, "She used to take twenty seeds of this, thirty pieces of that."

At this instant, the quality of the dream changes. When I awoke, the spoken phrase was clear in my mind, and I instantly connected the "thirty pieces of that" with thirty pieces of silver, the thirty pieces which Judas historically took to betray the man Jesus.

Upon waking, my feeling of having been betrayed by this gargantuan female was very strong in me. She represented the primitive, the integrated, the unselfconscious portion of myself which also had not particular concern for the agony I was currently undertaking of sorting out the masculine and feminine aspects of myself and the attempt to reintegrate these into a comfortably working whole.

In the dream it becomes night the instant these words are spoken; and, like the children Hansel and Gretel in the fairytale, my companion and I lay down to sleep. An unseen, but, thoughtful, someone throws a rough, warm blanket over us and the next scene takes place in the familiar battleground of my childhood home, "my mother's house." Someone, an anyone, is coming out the front door shouting, "They've moved the war office!"

As indeed they have as I come more into contact with the fears and hopes underlying my attempt at integration. It is like a battle which moves closer and closer to the front.

In the third and final scene of the dream, blond-haired Susan rides up on a bicycle. She is red-faced from her exertion, and mad.

The Susan is a real person, a friend of mine, who is every inch the typical Jewish *princess*, the little girl who is her father's darling and never needs to grow up. This particular person, however, long ago recognized the trap of the *princess* role, and had tried in many ways to break out of the confines of parental and familial approval, thus coercion, about how her life should be lived.

She, representing that part of me which is also the princess, rides up on her bicycle, the adolescent's vehicle, mad, and put out, that she has raced all this way only to find that the war office has been moved. The battle is not over, but at least the lines of demarcation have been more clearly outlined.

I must point out that, particularly in this type of dream which is so heavily allegorical, I feel that I play all of the roles from the *deus ex machina*, the observer, to the pouting Susan. This is what Jane Roberts in her books calls aspects of consciousness and what we must all deal with in order to become thoroughly integrated.

Friday, August 11, 1978—I am at a party at Anne's house. It is a bazaar for Mikey's new organization. There are a lot of people there and I go around looking at the items for sale.

Then I am in a corner with a group of people. A youngish man named Tony bends over and kisses me to show how much he loves me. There is some conversation. I am slightly embarrassed. Then Leonard, who has appeared on the other side of me, bends over and kisses me to show how much he loves me. I exclaim aloud in my delight and embarrassment. There is a flurry of exclamation and laughter and I think this is all aimed at me, but then someone at the front door says, "It's raining outside!"

I go out in the rain and bring in a very tiny (about the size of the palm of my hand) baby. I dry her off. She is fetus-sized but very perfectly formed.

Finally the baby, who is now older and larger, is standing with her father and older sister at the back door of my mother's house. They are going out to the bathroom.

In the final scene I hear a baby making loud noises and I discover that it is one of Bob Friedman's boys. I say to Bob that he must make the child behave or I will leave. Bob replies that he is only eight months old and can't be expected to behave yet.

Just like a grand finale, this dream contains elements of the whole week within it. It is not true that people's dreams always follow a theme so closely as these do like a fugue with point and counterpoint; nor are there necessarily so many types of dreams represented in one week; yet it must be remembered that at the beginning of the week I had determined to write this particular week of dreams down for this book.

The final dream begins with an event which leaves me feeling rejected and out of control. It is a bizarre bazaar and represents the fact that within the organization which I direct many people with whom I shared a great deal in the early days of the organization have left, including some of my closest friends. This has left a certain amount of anxiety within me that I may be doing the wrong thing. And in the dream itself I felt ill at ease and conspicuous.

Then, in the next segment of the dream I am surrounded by a crowd of friends. One of them, Tony, bends over and kisses me. This particular person is someone I knew years before during the post-college days when I was just beginning to find out who I was, as apart from the expectations of my family and others. He led what to me then represented the ultimate of romantic lives being an aide to a well-known civil rights lawyer in Washington, and that is what he represented in the dream—that aspect of myself.

Next Leonard, who represents home and marriage to me now, leaned over to kiss me. I cry out in delight and there is a loud burst of laughter and shouting. I think it is all directed at me, but for many of the people at the bazaar, it means their party is being ruined.

I go outside in the rain and rescue a tiny baby, who is perfectly formed, though much smaller than an ordinary infant. The symbolism of this tiny child is clear enough to be evident even to the novice in dream interpretation.

Born out of a gathering of present friends and acquaintances, at the moment of my being kissed by a former romantic symbol and by the individual who symbolizes my current home life, the baby represents the new me, the new self, which is being born out of the struggle to integrate male and female attributes. To some of the people at the party (who are also aspects of myself), the rain in which the baby is born indicates that the fun is over; but for me the child, though small, is "perfectly formed."

There follows in this dream an insight into two of the attitudes which I will have to work out toward this new selfhood. One is the view of the child, now grown older, standing with her father and older sister. It is unnecessary to discuss here all of the symbolism contained for me in this one picture except to say that, for me, the people who took the strongest roles in molding my sexual attitudes were my father and my older sister. I see this child, the new self, as still having to deal with the left-over feelings and attitudes developed in my childhood.

And finally, in the last scene of the dream, a baby (the same baby?) cries and I discover that it is the child of the individual who is chairman of the Board of Trustees of the organization which I direct. I say to him that he must make the child (the organization) behave itself or I will leave. He remarks that the baby is only eight months old (almost exactly the amount of time I had, in waking life, been dealing with the situation), and cannot yet be expected to behave perfectly—a statement which sums up my own impatience to behave "perfectly" and have the problem solved for once and for all.

To summarize, this week's worth of dreams may not be absolutely typical of all people and the way that all people dream. But, from my observation, it is certainly typical enough to demonstrate the variety of functions the dream life can perform and give some suggestions about how to deal effectively with dreams.

The dreams of this week ran the gamut from personal analysis and suggestion, to suggestions for other people, to visionary and lucid dreams. As the dreamer I had the choice of ignoring them or analyzing them, of using them to understand myself and my "reality" or thinking of them as just my imagination. There were dreams in this week which were purely uplifting, the native of the forest veld; and there were dreams which the bulk of dream literature chooses to ignore, saying that lucidity and direction of dream activity are impossible or imaginary. In all, the dreams of this week's worth of dreaming were commonplace, but more. They were suggestive of the fact that dreams occur in more than one area of space and time; that they deal with problems in a creative manner sometimes impossible to the waking state, bringing many factors into play; that it is possible through dreaming and through working with dreams, to achieve yet "undreamed-of" awareness.

Chapter Ten

Beyond Dreaming

To go beyond dreaming is to go beyond the ordinary defini-tion of dreams as nighttime movies, however helpful they may be. Beyond dreaming is the acceptance of a theory that reality may be more than we ordinarily perceive it to be and that dreams may be a very valid and important part of that reality, gaining in value as we give them credence. This is a theory, of course, and should be treated as such; but a theory which can be explored by the adven-turesome individual, alone or in the company of others.

In order to aid you on your adventure into the territory of dreams, I would like to give you some exercises which I have culled from my own reading and my own experiences and which have been used with some degree of satisfaction by students in classes and workshops I have taught, by myself, and by some of my friends. The keyword to this sort of exploration, like any other type of experiment or adventure, is balance. On one side of the territory generally defined as dreams lies normalcy and the ordinary world; on the other lies that area sometimes defined as madness, overactive imagination or hallucination. The explorer forges into unknown territory while keeping strong ties with known territory. Likewise the dream adventurer goes on his journey with the balance of proper diet, healthy exercise, and a relatively untroubled waking life; a good companion on either voyage is well worth having. The true scientist, while keeping an open mind, is not satisfied if an experiment works only once or twice, but instead wants a result which is repeatable and can be verified by fellow scientists. In the study of dreams as well, any theory which can be postulated about the meaning or use of dreaming must be repeatable and verifiable. Yet unlike their more substantive counterparts such as metals or ores, dreams occur (even when studied in laboratories) first in the laboratory of the human mind; so look around yourself, feel the limits of your laboratory, and prepare for the adventure into inner space.

First Steps—Flexibility

For most of us the unexpected doesn't happen primarily because we give it no space in which to happen. Ordered lives tend to produce ordered experiences, or experiences which we sometimes tend to ignore because they happen as regularly as breathing. Do not get me wrong. I am not suggesting that you completely reorder your life. Balance, remember? What I am suggesting, however, are a few simple exercises which will disorder to some minor extent some minor part of your life; but which may well provide a nudge to dreaming and experimenting. The first thing in any change of pattern is to become more flexible, just as the gymnast limbers up or the touch typist first learns simple exercises for formerly unused muscles.

1. Break the pattern

Earlier I noted that breaking the sleep pattern was very helpful to me in exploring dreaming, and especially lucid dreaming. Some people tell me that it is utterly impossible for them to change their own sleeping patterns since, "the baby is up at 7 a.m. no matter what I do," or "the house is just too noisy for an afternoon or evening nap," or "I have to fix dinner when I get home from work." To many of these people I reply that perhaps if they asked for some cooperation or got other members of the family involved in the adventures of dreaming, it might indeed be possible to change the sleep patterns, not only for themselves but their entire families. How many children do you know, for example, who don't want to take a nap because "big kids don't take naps," but who might like to sleep in the afternoon if dreaming became an adventure discussed by the entire family?

However, I am willing to admit that some people's schedules simply do not allow for much rearrangement. There are other things which can be done to allow the patterns of flexibility to creep into one's life and these are a few of the suggestions I would like to make. Remember that in order for an experimenter to allow for the results of an experiment, it is necessary to keep an open mind rather than determining in advance what the results of the experiment are going to be; and in the case of the perception of reality as more than we have ordinarily perceived it, or as more flexible and interconnected than we have ordinarily perceived it, it is necessary to give ourselves an arena in which the perceptions can occur rather than maintaining every action of old habit patterns and then declaring the experiment invalid.

2. Take Yourself to Lunch

For some people, the change toward a more flexible view of the world can begin with some very ordinary act which is not habitual or which is outside of the ordinary habit pattern. Instead of eating lunch in the cafeteria with the rest of the staff, one day take yourself out to lunch—alone, to the park or a quiet restaurant. Watch the people, think, daydream. Give yourself a break. Or, if you're the part of the family which stays at home, give yourself a piece of time in which you are not to be disturbed. Plan no work for that time, just relaxation and enjoyment. Absolutely nothing may happen the first time you try either of these exercises (you think Toscanini became expert the first time he played music?); but try the same thing a few days later, and again in a day or two.

Begin to set slight changes in your routine and see what happens, just that easily, to your dreaming patterns. Record your experiments, and don't give up after the first try, or even the first hundred trys. Try jogging or exercise at an unaccustomed time; try a walk at night with a friend; and perhaps try, over a period of time, to catch a nap in the afternoon or early evening.

3. Try out your senses

Just as most of us allow our life routines to become habitual, so do most of us allow the experiences given to our ordinary five senses to become so patterned that we barely are aware of them. It is my contention that that group of people known in our society as artists or creative thinkers, may have gotten that way not because of any talent peculiar just to them, but because they allowed themselves or were allowed flexibility of the senses. And if you read, as I have, the lives of many of these creative individuals, you will find that the incidence of what we call dreams or visions or extraordinary experiences, is extremely high. What's the secret: I think it is relatively simple. They have trained and stimulated their senses to perceive beyond the habitual. Here are some exercises you might like to try:

See the Spaces, Hear the Silence

This particular exercise can be done anywhere from a crowded subway train to a quiet park. I generally recommend that students try it first in some place quiet, and first with seeing because most people use their sight more than other senses and relative silence often leads to less distraction. However, this is not entirely necessary. Choose an ordinary object, say a tree. Ordinarily we look at a tree by perhaps noticing a branch, looking at the leaves, following the line of the branch with our eyes down to the point where the branch meets the tree trunk and sometimes giving ourselves the verbal message, "tree." This time, when you look at the tree, look not at the branch or leaves or trunk but the space formed by these. In other words, look at space as contained by form.

Perform another exercise. Ordinarily when we listen to sound, we listen for the familiar—the hum of the refrigerator, the noise of traffic, the children playing in the yard next door. This time, just for a few minutes, listen to the silence between these sounds, listen to the space contained by the more ordinary sounds in our lives. It is a way of looking, a way of hearing, which heightens and trains our perceptions.

Look Both Ways

When you were younger, you may have done, as many people I know did, eye exercises designed for strengthening a weak or astigmatic eye. These exercises were somewhat disorienting and, overdone, may have given a headache or made you slightly nauseous. However, it is part of my theory of dreaming and dream perception that one element of the reason we do not see the extraordinary in the ordinary is because most of us have trained our senses only so far. We have, so to speak, allowed the muscles of perception to become atrophied or rigid. For most of us, nausea is in some way connected with fear, and one of the greatest fears in any society is being "different," or being able to perceive things which are "just your imagination." To this end, I urge anyone who is seriously interested in experimenting with the dream reality to undertake these exercises for training the senses beyond their usual habit patterns.

Take a walk, anywhere you would ordinarily take a walk. Usually you walk with your eyes straight ahead, right? Or focused on the ground in front of you, diverted occasionally by a look to see what made a particular sound or who is coming across the street.

This time, harken back to those old eye exercises. Allow your eyes to sweep the horizon from the far right of your peripheral vision to the far left. Keep walking. At first you may become dizzy, even nauseous. Don't stop immediately. Don't worry about falling over your feet. Most of us have a built in sense of balance which keeps us gravitating normally. But *do* extend these periods of walking with the eyes sweeping the horizon. Walk as swiftly as possible. If possible, carry no burdens, but allow the shoulders to relax and the arms to swing freely at the sides of the body. Exercise your senses past the ordinary ways of perceiving.

When you have had enough of this particular exercise for a few moments, and you are still walking, allow yourself to examine your surroundings. Look at the leaf on the sidewalk. Look at the elderly gentleman in the doorway, the way he stands. Feel the texture of the fur of the stray dog who comes up to be petted. Then return to the eye exercise.

What does all of this have to do with dreaming? Nothing directly, as I've said. But the experimenter who enters into an experiment with a certainty of what the result will be, prejudices, to some extent, the results of the experiment; and the dream experimenter who enters the world of dream perception, certain that the ordinary ways of perceiving are the only ways, that dreams are dreams and nothing more, prejudices to some extent the possible result of that experiment in perception. Become flexible. Be alert.

Second Steps—Symbols

Everyone who has studied dreams to any extent is aware of the fact that dreams are said to occur in the language of symbols—that whatever event appears in the dream is quite likely to symbolize some fear, anxiety, hope, wish, or aspiration on the part of the dreamer. And part of the value of traditional dream analysis has been to make the connections between these hopes or fears or aspirations and the events of the dream world in order that the dreamer might come to a better understanding of self. There is undeniable value in this, and undeniable value in self-knowledge.

The connection, however, which is not frequently made, is that events and objects of the ordinary waking world are also highly symbolic in much the same way of events and objects in the dream world, and if treated in the same manner might yield the same results.

The problem lies, I think, in our definition of the word symbol. Years of teaching high school students, if they did nothing else for me at all, showed me that no matter how many times we would go over the simplest definition of symbol as "something which stands for or takes the place of something else," invariably when it came time to give an example of a symbol the student would point to "that image in a poem" (i.e. Spring-like yellow daffodils) or "that thing that happens in a dream."

Only rarely would any student make the connection that a word is a symbol for an idea or object; or that an ordinary object such as a pencil could symbolize as many thoughts, feelings, or emotions as there were students in the room. In other words, I believe we tend to look at symbols as something connected with the extraordinary—the dream, the poem, the creative event; and ignore the fact that ordinary objects, ideas and events are symbolic. Again we draw the line between the ordinary and the extraordinary, the dream world and "reality." Perhaps we have been taught to do so by our formalized study of literature which from an early age sets the writer or creative thinker apart from the ordinary individual. But if it is something we have been taught, I feel it is something we should unlearn. For it creates a boundary line that does not exist. The act of examining the symbolic content of ordinary objects or events in our lives leads us rather quickly to the conclusion that everything, or almost everything, around us is symbolic or representative of some inner thought, desire or feeling—which in turn gives us a clue to how creative we really are on an inner level, in the broadest sense of the word creative. Here are some exercises you might like to try.

1. Talk to A Plant

In earlier chapters, I talked about the technique of gestalting dream information as a valuable help to understanding the meaning of a dream. As you recall, the technique of gestalting provides that the individual call up a mental image of a person or object from a dream and then carry on a conversation with that person or object in which questions are asked or answered.

This same technique can be used in waking life with equally valid and valuable results. Because some people fell uncomfortable with the idea of carrying on an imaginary conversation with an object in their daily environment even if that conversation is never verbalized (this is sometimes called animating inanimate objects and described by cultural anthropologists as one of those things which distinguish our civilized culture from other more "uncivilized" cultures—the latter being those who animate inanimate objects), I have given you an easy object to start out with.

Given today's gardening craze, most people keep at least one plant around the house, if not a whole gardenful. Plants have been studied for some time by a wide variety of specialists and are believed to have some degree of sentience, so maybe you could just make believe that your plant was talking back in tones too low to hear.

I would like you to do the following. Sit down beside a chosen plant. Ask it the following questions. Why are you here? What meaning do you have to me? Are you happy here? Is there anything I can do for you?

The answers may be a little bit slow in formulating themselves, especially if this is the first time you've played this sort of game; but I can almost assure you that there will be answers there, that the answers will just pop into your head and you won't even have to think much about them. Write the answers down. Look at them. What do they tell you about yourself? That is the symbolic content of the plant for you.

2. Talk to Another Object

Now that that is out of the way, you are beginning to get some idea of how things in our ordinary waking life can be and are symbolic to us and can even symbolize things we weren't aware of in ourselves much as dreams do.

Choose another object, perhaps a favorite piece of china or an ottoman you dislike and keep tripping over. Ask it the same four questions. Why are you here? What meaning do you have to me? Are you happy here? Is there anything I can do for you? Listen to the answers. This time you may have to work a little harder. You may feel you are "making it all up" or "acting foolish," but remember these are exercises for the imagination, warm-up exercises for the senses we seldom exercise. Don't make a big thing of it, but write the answers down. Look at them. See what they tell you about yourself. That is the symbolic content of those objects for you.

3. Talk to An Event

And finally, we reach the toughest one of all—the one which requires the most sensitivity and imagination. Take an event from your daily life, perhaps an event which has been troubling you, and treat it as if it were a dream.

Perhaps there has been someone troubling you at work or you had a run-in with the boss. Maybe there is a person who is particularly attractive to you or you have just had a nice time with a group of friends. Whatever the event you choose, treat it just as you would a dream. Try the same gestalting techniques on it that you would on a dream and see what happens.

You might like to start with the same four questions that you began with in the above exercise. Remember, this is a gestalting technique, an imaginary conversation. No fair asking the persons in the real-life event how they would answer the question; rather, try to imagine how they would answer.

Don't forget the objects in the event. Just as in the dream an object may contain symbolic significance, so might the objects in a waking event. Write your answers down. Think about them. You are now learning the symbolic significance of people and objects in your daily life, how they relate to your inner thoughts and desires and wishes. For you, as for many others, this may be a very revealing process and may begin to demonstrate how integrally linked we really are with all of the people and things in our ordinary waking lives.

Third Step—Visualization

The next step in going beyond dreaming is one which, like the preceding steps, can be taken by anyone whether or not "dreams" are recalled every night by the score, infrequently, or not at all.

In every dream study or workshop in which I am involved, students are given a series of exercises called guided meditations or visualizations. There is no hocus-pocus in this. In the ancient yogic tradition meditation is known as the ability to focus one's attention away from the world we ordinarily perceive as the exterior and toward the world we ordinarily perceive as interior. That is to say that, for anyone, much of what makes up daily life is not our interaction with people and objects around us, but interior events known variously as memory, fantasy, imagination, vision, theorizing, daydreaming, and dreaming—to name a few.

And the name of the game is focus. Most of the time our minds are filled with an endless clatter of input from what's for lunch to what the boss can do with this load of paperwork. Seldom is the input organized and seldom do we deal with even a fraction of it. Yet the entire concept of recalling dreams and even going beyond what we generally label as dreaming is based on the ability to focus one's attention on an "interior" event. Thus, in addition to whatever insight might come from these exercises, they are a practical lesson in learning to focus. There are as many guided meditations as there are people to create them, and you may already be familiar with one or two of these; but here are three exercises which I use presently with students:

Find a comfortable chair or relax on the couch. Take your shoes off. Loosen your clothes or wear loose fitting clothes. Generally these meditations are guided by a leader who gives directions while the student sits or lies comfortably, but this is not entirely necessary. You may want to find someone to read the exercises to you; or you can actually read them to yourself. Keep outside noises to a minimum and try to arrange it so you will not be interrupted by loud noises such as dogs barking, the telephone ringing or someone knocking at the door.

1. A Trip Up The Mountain
This is the oldest and best-known of these exercises, used often as a psychological test.
Imagine that you are in a house of your own construction. It does not have to be the house in which you currently live, but can be your dream house. Look out the window. Note what the windows are like.

Open the front door and, in your imagination, go outside. Look at your surroundings. What are they like?

There is a path which leads away from the house. Take the path. Go for a walk in your imagination, still noticing what your surroundings are like. You meet an animal on the path. What kind of an animal is it? How does it act? Greet the animal and continue on your way.

Your path is blocked by a barrier. What kind of barrier is it? How do you circumvent the barrier? The path continues and so do you.

Finally, you come to a body of water. You cross the water. What kind of water is it and how do you get across?

On the other side of the water the path continues and there is a mountain. You begin to climb the mountain. Climb slowly. Look around you. The path takes you through various areas of the mountain until at last you reach the top. At the top of the mountain, overlooking all that can be seen, is another structure, also built by you. Enter it and sit quietly for a few moments. What kind of a structure is it?

Finally, you return—back down the mountainside, down the path across the water, past the barrier, greeting the animal, back to your dream house.

At the end of this, or any other similar session, you may feel slightly disoriented and you may want to give yourself a suggestion such as, "I am returning to ordinary consciousness—awake, refreshed and fully relaxed." Try not to get up too suddenly and allow yourself a few minutes to switch from interior to exterior focus.

If, for the above exercise, you were to write down your responses to the questions before they went out of your head, you would find that you might learn quite a lot about yourself by responding to some fairly commonly agreed-upon symbols. In the psychological testing (as well as in ordinary dream analysis) the house of this exercise is taken to represent the personality (for example: a tiny cottage, a person with old fashioned values) and the windows, the person's outlook on life. Someone with tiny, narrow windows may want to close out the world while the individual with large picture windows may be expansive and gregarious. This continues through the rest of the exercise. The path symbolizes the path through life; the animal, the way one sees one's animal or physical self. The barrier represents the way the individual meets obstacles in life. The water indicates the emotional self; and crossing it, the way one deals with one's emotions. The mountain, of course, is the spiritual self; and the structure at the top, the type of sprititual edifice one has built.

Generally people find this exercise to be quite revealing even when it's repeated again and again if they are honest with themselves and don't try to force the images into something they'd like to see rather than what they feel.

However, for the point of this chapter it is sufficient to try to do the exercise; to try to focus the attention on the world of the interior; and see how, in fact, we are creating symbols all of the time in a process that is very like dreaming.

2. A Dream Teacher

The second exercise is a little more complex than the first because I want you to go to the place where dreams come from.

Here is the way I generally present it to students when we do a guided meditation:

I want you to go to the place where dreams come from, to the vast continent known as your interior. Find a method of transportation. It may be a boat, or a plane, or a bicycle, or you may prefer to walk there, but find whatever method of transportation you'd like and let's begin to travel.

Look over the dreamscape. You know it because you come here often whether you remember it or not. Look at the population and the things that grow here. This is the land of your dreams.

Now somewhere in this land, someplace that you know very well, lives a very wise person. It may be on a mountaintop or it may be in a valley, but you know the place because you come here often. I want you to go now to find that wise individual.

Stand before that wise person. Look and remember well. You have met before. Listen. This wise friend has something to tell you. Listen carefully. Pay attention. You will remember clearly everything that is said.

Now become that wise friend. In fact, you are one and the same.

Returning now from the land of dreams, the place where dreams come from, remember this person. Remember what has been said. Remember who you are. Get on your vehicle, your plane or train, return now past the dream landscape. You may want to repeat to yourself the previously given suggestion about being awake and refreshed.

If you had difficulty with the suggestion of becoming the wise person, ask yourself why. Remember that in dreams anyone we meet is, at some level, ourselves, or an aspect of ourself.

3. A Dream Object

And finally, here is an exercise which I frequently use with students in creative writing classes. If you have the temptation to say things like this is nonsense; these exercises are time-wasting; I don't have time for such things, remember that, like any other disciplined study, the rewards gained are likely to be in direct proportion to the amount of time and effort expended. Dreams and the world of the interior can indeed be elusive, but no more elusive than the home run is to the beginning baseball player. Quite simply, we often think that work which produces results in the exterior world is more valuable than that which produces results in the interior—and, as a possible byproduct, results in the exterior.

This is an exercise which can do both.

The beginning and ending are the same as the preceding exercise, finding a means of transportation, going to the place where dreams come from. This time I want you to park your vehicle somewhere, anywhere (or if you are on foot, stand still) and look around you. Find an object which catches your eye. Walk around it. Examine it from all sides. Feel the object, its texture. Listen to it.

Now, because objects in the world of dreams don't have quite the same properties as objects in the waking world, no matter what the size and shape of this object, you will have absolutely no difficulty picking it up.

Pick up the object. Return to your vehicle, and bring the object back with you, back from the land of dreams.

Now that you've returned, if you want to really complete this exercise, you may want to sit down and write about it, write a complete description. Don't hamper yourself unnecessarily with form. You may want to write a poem; or, if the object was of a certain type, you may want to write a song, or possibly you'd like to paint a picture of it.

Whatever the other results of these exercises, by this time, if you have done them, though we haven't analyzed a single dream or even talked about dreams per se, you will have begun to experience first hand how we tend to set boundaries between waking and sleeping, dreaming and not-dreaming. And hopefully you will have, by yourself, begun to set aside or remove some of these boundaries. For as long as we maintain the line which says on this side is reality, being awake, being sane; and on that side is unreality, being asleep, dreaming, we cannot hope to go beyond dreaming.

Final Steps—Going Beyond

There are some neat tricks about dreaming which most of the people I meet say they can't do; but which they'd like to do. One of these is precognitive dreams or dream telepathy. The other is lucid dreaming.

1. Dream Telepathy

For this set of exercises, you will need at least one accomplice, and more if you can find them. I suggest that you either ask them to read this book or that you describe what you have read so that you are beginning with a somewhat similar background.

People often tell me that they never have telepathic, precognitive or psychic experiences in their dream state (let alone the waking state); but I believe we are hampered by two major obstacles: one, the definition of telepathic communication, and two, the fact that we seldom discuss dreams with other people. For these exercises it will be necessary to redefine, to some extent, telepathy; and to communicate with someone or someones about your dreams.

First, the definition of telepathy. Most people tend to define telepathy (if they think about it at all) as a direct, one-to-one correlation of events between two individuals in which communication takes place by other than ordinary means—no telephone conversation, letter or telegram, just the contact between one mind and another.

So far, so good. Yet it is my contention that telepathy takes place one hundred percent of the time, even though it is seldom recognized. One problem is our lack of experience and attention. We tend not to notice when the extraordinary takes place because we expect the ordinary.

The other is our lack of awareness of the symbolic content of our daily lives, either in the dream state or the waking state. This gets to be a little tricky, and I'd like for you at least to give it some careful consideration.

Have you ever seen an object, perhaps a yellow rose, and said, "That reminds me of my grandmother?"; or heard an old tune and remembered a first date or an old friend? Now what you were receiving was first the *symbol* for the person or event and not the person or event itself.

Dreams operate in much the same way, except, if anything, more flexibly. I recently participated in a series of dream communication experiments with a group of friends. One of the intentions of this experiment was to see if we could dream about each other; another was to see if we could lucid dream together.

During the first in the series of experiments, several members of the group dreamed about houses, not one house but a group of houses. Because these people were fairly skilled in dream interpretation independently they came to the conclusion that the houses might represent the members of the group and how they felt about the houses might be their feelings toward other members of the group.

It gets to be a little tricky, doesn't it? As a group, these people dreamed about houses. Left to their own devices, if they'd been asked if they dreamed about Ellen or Steve, they might have said, no. But because *several* members of the group dreamed about houses, and the house is traditionally a symbol for the individual, it was fairly easy to determine that the people may well have been dreaming about one another. This is the same phenomenon that occurs when you see the rose. The rose is not your grandmother. It simply reminds you of, or is a symbol for, your grandmother.

Obviously, within this type of a system, the number of factors we're dealing with increases dramatically. It's easy to say that anything equals anything else and we're all dreaming about one another all of the time. That is not what I'm suggesting.

What I am suggesting is that you find another person or persons and begin to compare dreams with them. You might begin by simply discussing what dreams you have and becoming familiar with one another's symbols.

Then you might set a series of tasks for yourselves. You might see if you can meet each other in the dream state, not once but at least three or four times. Then get together and discuss the dreams you had on those particular occasions. You may find that you met each and every time. Great. You're ready for some other type of work.

But chances are you might have had more problems than that. You might have appeared in one another's dreams as your automobile or a favorite book if at all. You might have dreamed each other, but doing totally different things. Or, and this is a common one, you might have dreamed each other quite clearly, but not at the appointed dream time.

In my opinion, this type of behavior is only natural for beginning dreamers. The exception is the person who can step right in and communicate in this way all of the time.

Precognition fits in to the same category as telepathy. Again, I think we are often aware, through our dreams and other perceptions, of what may happen in the so-called future. But, again, it tends to escape our notice because it is couched in symbolic terms or mixed in with other perceptions.

If you will recall, one of the exercises given for people who wanted to remember their dreams and could not, was to think during the preceding day about dream recall, to give the suggestion just before sleeping that dreams would be recalled, and to make it as convenient as possible for recall to happen. I think the same holds true for dream precognition and telepathy.

In order to experience clear telepathic and precognitive dreams on a regular basis, it is helpful to pre-program the experience by thinking about it during the day and suggesting it before sleep. It is necessary to give the experience a chance to work by recording dream events as they happen and seeing if they "come true," and by giving enough time to discussion and experiment with dreams with other people to discover whether telepathy occurs. The reason, I think, that people often feel they don't have these types of psychic experiences is that the experiences most frequently noted and also discussed in books are the more dramatic experiences such as the foretelling of death or accident. Little notice is paid to the fact that we may know in advance what Mom will bring home from the grocery store.

2. Lucid Dreaming

Since an entire chapter was devoted to a description of lucid dreaming, there is no need to go into that here. But lucid dreaming is another of those feats which the ordinary dreamer often feels is impossible. There are several techniques which can be employed to achieve the lucid dream state and I will describe some of them here.

Probably the easiest and least taxing way is the one described in the earlier chapter, that of simply become aware, while in the dream state, that one is dreaming and then maintaining the awareness.

It takes some practice, but as far as I can determine can be achieved by almost anyone. The trick is to simply notice some irregularity in the "reality" of the dream state, some incongruity if you will, and recognize that this is a dream. Then focus on an object or some part of the body which is always with you, and expand that focus to the rest of the dream reality while maintaining the awareness of dreaming. That done, it is possible to travel, to visit friends, to fly, or to do any number of other things while maintaining the awareness of the dream.

Another technique for achieving this lucid state, and one employed by yogis for centuries as well as by other people not trained in yogic practices, is to enter this lucid state from waking reality.

To do this it is best to lie down and relax the body. Then there are a number of techniques which can be employed. One is to breathe deeply, and normally, focusing attention on the breathing and maintaining that focus. On each exhaled breath, notice the slight pause before inhalation. *This pause is the lucid state.* The more relaxed the body becomes, the longer this pause will become until finally one enters a full state of lucidity.

Now one may experience almost immediately in this state some sensations which can be disturbing or encourage a return to waking consciousness. There may be the feeling of floating or rising out of the bed or body. There may be a tingling sensation in the extremities or a slight pain in the head or the feeling of coming out of one's head. This is generally attributable to the fear we have of doing the extraordinary, and I suggest that you try to maintain your focus on breathing.

There are some other ways you may also focus. One is to imagine a ball of light in front of your closed eyes. As you watch, this globe of light will slowly change colors going from red to orange to yellow to green to blue to pale blue and then white. As the globe of light becomes white and then opaque and then clear, white light, you are likely to experience the same sensations described above.

The real challenge is to learn to focus because if, in fact, waking reality is only one part of the broad spectrum of consciousness upon which we can focus our attention, it is certainly also true that it is that part of the spectrum upon which we habitually and intently focus our attention. In order to focus our attention somewhere else, and somewhere that has often been described to us as scary or crazy, we will certainly first have to learn how to refocus our attention and then learn how to control that focus.

You can see that by now we have slipped into the realms that are quite regularly called not-dreaming or beyond dreaming.

What are the practical purposes of such a step? Being a practical person myself, I always like to know what good something is going to do me and what useful value it has before I decide whether to do it.

Well, quite outside of any uses to which going beyond dreaming might be put at the present moment, it must be understood that we know almost nothing about the vase expanse called consciousness; know almost nothing about the brain and how it functions; and, aside from the small amount of esoteric metaphysical and occult literature printed in each generation, have relatively few speculations about what might be the yield from exploration of this vast area.

Some of the certain implications of dream experiments and experiments in consciousness already conducted are that it is quite possible to communicate over vast distances without use of the known physical means; that it is possible to have a vast and accurate knowledge of oneself, and that from that knowledge, creativity can grow in yet unexpected quantities; that at some level of awareness, sometimes touched by dreams, consciousness is aware of the physical needs of the body before they are manifested in illness or accident, and willing to give us the information through dreams.

Through dreaming and practice of that skill it is possible to sift through, sort out, and organize into a manageable unit what may now seem to be a vast and incoherent complex of symbols which contain information about our personal universe and even, perhaps, the known and unknown exterior galaxy. Not bad for a few pleasant hours of dreaming? But perhaps needing a training and practice we have yet to put into effect.

And now I would like to ask you a most extraordinary and unauthorlike thing. I know that authors are supposed to put out their books with a simple eye to the information. They are not supposed to, particularly, care how they are read or by whom. But, as you can see from these pages, dreams are a particular interest of mine. I, too, am always looking for the person with whom I can share the unique and vastly amusing contents of my dreams and speculations about their contents.

I would like to hear fom you. I would like to hear whether you try suggestions made in this book, and with what results. I would like to hear about your own dream experiments and the questions they might raise for you.

Because I am sure that there is no laboratory in the country or in the world that is now trying to find the limits of dreaming—and go beyond those limits. The only laboratory is yourself, and the far reaches of your dreams.

Remember to approach them with the balanced and questioning mind of the scientist and the adventuresome spirit of the explorer.

Bibliography

Capra, Fritjof. *The Tao of Physics.* Berkeley: Shambhala, 1975.

Donahoe, James J. *Dream Reality.* Oakland, California: Bench Press, 1974.

Faraday, Ann. *Dream Power.* New York: Berkeley Medallion Books/Berkeley Publishing, 1973.

_____ *The Dream Game,* AFAR Publishers, 1974.

Fort, Charles. *Lo!* New York: ACE Books, 1941.

Fox, Oliver. *Astral Projection.* New Hyde Park, New York: University Books, 1962.

Garfield, Patricia. *Creative Dreaming.* New York: Ballantine Books, 1976.

Grant, Joan. *The Eyes of Horus.* New York: Avon Books, 1969.

_____ with Denys Kelsey. *Many Lifetimes.* Garden City, New York: Doubleday, 1967.

Jenks, Kathleen. *Journey of a Dream Animal.* New York: Julian Press, 1975.

Jung, Carl. *Memories, Dreams, Reflections.* New York: Random House, 1961.

Lilly, John C. *The Center of the Cyclone.* New York: Bantam, 1972.

Masters, Robert and Jean Houston. *Mind Games.* New York: Dell, 1972.

Monroe, Robert A. *Journeys Out of the Body.* Garden City, New York: Anchor Press/Doubleday, 1973.

Neihardt, John. *Black Elk Speaks.* New York: Morrow & Co., 1932.

Reed, Henry, ed. *Sundance Community Dream Journal.* Virginia Beach, Virginia, A.R.E. Press.

Roberts, Jane. *The Nature of Personal Reality.* New York: Prentice-Hall, 1974.

_____ *Psychic Politics.* New York: Prentice-Hall, 1976.

_____ *Seth Speaks.* New York: Prentice-Hall, 1972.

Sonnet, Andre. *The Twilight Zone of Dreams.* New York: Chilton Company Book Division, 1961.

Tart, Charles T., ed. *Altered States of Consciousness.* Garden City, New York: Anchor Books/Doubleday, 1972.

Tolkien, J.R.R. *The Tolkien Reader.* New York: Ballantine, 1964.

Ullman, Montague and Stanley Krippner with Alan Vaughn. *Dream Telepathy.* New York: Macmillan, 1973.

White, Stewart Edward. *Across the Unknown.* New York: E.P. Dutton, 1939.

Yogananda, Paramahansa. *Autobiography of a Yogi.* Los Angeles: Self Realization Fellowship, 1977.

Jean Campbell

Jean Campbell is executive director of Poseida Institute, a Virginia Beach-based organization devoted to research and education in the subject of parapsychology. Director at the institute since 1976, she has been a member of the Poseidia board of directors since its 1973 incorporation.

A popular TV talk show guest, Jean frequently lectures and teaches classes on dreams. She spends several hours weekly talking with ordinary dreamers as well as practicing psychics on the nature and revelance of dreams. At least one hour of her weekly radio program "Psychic Dimensions" is devoted to dreams, with calls from the listening audience.

Dreams Beyond Dreaming is Jean's second book. She ghost-authored *Great Gardens of America,* a book about edible wild plants in the late 1960s.

Dreaming is a way of life for Jean who feels that when an individual stops dreaming, he or she stops growing.

The Unilaw Library Series

Unilaw Library is a line of inspirational, metaphysical and religious books which demonstrate the basic compatability of classic religious principles with ancient and modern metaphysical cosmology. The line will include fiction, children's books and practical, self-help applications. The purpose of Unilaw Library is to draw from all disciplines which contribute to the evolution of human thought, from the latest scientific discoveries to the re-thinking of old dogmas and attitudes which will lead humanity to the truth about the nature of life and the universe.